Design as a Catalyst for Learning

MEREDITH DAVIS • PETER HAWLEY • BERNARD MCMULLAN • GERTRUDE SPILKA

Association for Supervision and Curriculum Development
Alexandria, Virginia USA

Association for Supervision and Curriculum Development
1250 N. Pitt Street • Alexandria, Virginia 22314-1453 USA
Telephone: 1-800-933-2723 or 703-549-9110 • Fax: 703-299-8631
Web site: http://www.ascd.org • E-mail: member@ascd.org

Gene R. Carter, *Executive Director*
Michelle Terry, *Assistant Executive Director, Program Development*
Nancy Modrak, *Director, Publishing*
John O'Neil, *Acquisitions Editor*
Julie Houtz, *Managing Editor of Books*
Kathie Felix, *Associate Editor*
Mary Beth Nielsen, *Assistant Editor*
René Bahrenfuss, *Copy Editor*
Charles D. Halverson, *Project Assistant*
Gary Bloom, *Director, Editorial, Design, and Production Services*
Karen Monaco, *Senior Designer*
Tracey A. Smith, *Production Manager*
Dina Murray, *Production Coordinator*
John Franklin, *Production Coordinator*

Designed by Grafik Communications, Ltd.
Cover Design by Karen Monaco

Printed in the United States of America.

ASCD Stock No.: 197022
ASCD member price: $28.95   nonmember price: $34.95

December 1997 member book (p). ASCD Premium, Comprehensive, and Regular members
periodically receive ASCD books as part of their membership benefits. No. FY98-3

Library of Congress Cataloging-in-Publication Data

Design as a catalyst for learning / Meredith Davis ... [et al.].
    p. cm.

Papers based on research conducted by the OMG Center for
Collaborative Learning.
Includes bibliographical references (p.).
ISBN 0-87120-284-0 (pb)

1. Creative thinking—Study and teaching—United States. 2. Design—Study
and teaching—United States. 3. Problem-solving—Study and teaching—
United States. 4. Active learning—United States. 5. Curriculum planning—
United States. 6. Educational change—United States. I. Davis, Meredith
(Meredith J.)

LB1062.D475   1997
370.15'2–dc21   97-43361
                                                  CIP

01 00 99 98 97   5 4 3 2 1

Table of Contents

The Design as a Catalyst for Learning project was funded through a
cooperative agreement (DCA 93-08) from the National Endowment for
the Arts, a federal agency. The initial project research was conducted
by Gertrude J. Spilka, principal researcher, Bernard McMullen, and Lisa
Nutter of the OMG Center for Collaborative Learning in Philadelphia, Pa.

Foreword

this book speaks directly to educators, but I believe it holds insights that will be of interest to parents and business leaders as well. In his 1997 State of American Education address, U.S. Secretary of Education Richard W. Riley reminded us that as we approach the 21st century, "nothing should be more important to us as a nation than the actions we take now to help our young people prepare for the future."[1] As a mother, I know what all parents want for their children: to give them every opportunity to reach their full potential. We want our children to know how to work well with other people. We want them to feel competent in solving the problems they may encounter at work and in the community. Above all, we want them to be happy and engaged in life, to know how to keep learning, enjoying, and contributing.

Goal Three of our National Education Goals, endorsed by the nation's governors and both parties in Congress, summarizes these desires well. After stating that all children should graduate from high school with a firm understanding of core subjects including math, science, social studies *and the arts* it continues ". . . and every school in America will ensure that all students learn to use their minds well, so that they may be prepared for responsible

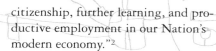

citizenship, further learning, and productive employment in our Nation's modern economy."[2]

The world into which students now graduate is changing rapidly as global competition increases and information technology transforms the way work is conducted. Where once the "three R's" were sufficient for most young people to gain entry into the workforce, today they are only the foundation for a set of higher-level thinking and performance skills sought by employers. The "knowledge worker" now in demand is a person who works well in a team,

particularly with people from different cultural backgrounds. Such workers also know how to access, evaluate, interpret, and communicate information in a variety of media. They have the curiosity and creativity to pose questions and to innovate. They can grasp the dynamic relationships among parts that constitute larger systems. They know how to allocate human and material resources to get things done on time and to high standards of quality.

We need these skills in all spheres of our society: in government, business, and the nonprofit sector. The quality of everyday life in our communities as well as the nation's economic vitality depend upon people's ability to view problems from many perspectives, to construct creative approaches to solving them, and to evaluate those solutions with a critical eye. Such skills lie at the heart of engaged, responsible citizenship. They are also fundamental to the innovations that stimulate entrepreneurship and job growth.

How then do we develop these skills in our children? What kind of schools can nurture them? I am convinced—and an increasing number of business and civic leaders are too—that education in the arts is an essential component. This was illustrated last year in a special education supplement published by *Business Week* magazine.[3] There, business

and civic leaders gave testimony to the value of the arts in developing the kinds of well-rounded, hard-working, innovative performers they are seeking.

They know that, in any art form, the artist is concerned with both process and end product. Design, the subject of this book, is a good example. Whether the objective is a product, a building, a city plan, or a graphic communication, when children are engaged in the process of designing, they are learning to identify needs, frame problems, work collaboratively, explore and appreciate the contexts within which a solution must work, weigh alternatives, and communicate their ideas verbally, graphically, and in three dimensions.

Design is also about making and doing as a way of knowing, of really understanding the abstract concepts taught in schools. It's about putting ideas to work in situations that allow children to test themselves and the value of learning in everyday life. Engaging in periodic self-assessment and critiques of work in progress, students come to understand that performance testing to high standards and continual improvement are fundamental to the process, in lifelong learning no less than in design.

Dance, theatre, music, and the visual arts share many of these characteristics and should be part of any comprehensive educational program. Design is in a unique position, however, because the very "stuff" of design is all around children: in the classroom, the neighborhood, and even in the virtual worlds available on the Internet. As the teachers you will meet in this book reveal, the very fact that the products of design are so ubiquitous and so tangible makes design itself an easy hook to capture students' attention, a natural path on which to set them exploring how the world works and how they can make a difference in it.

These teachers also will tell you that design helps students integrate knowledge from other disciplines and motivates them to attend school. Given that truancy costs the United States some $228 billion a year and corporations spend an additional $30 billion annually on the remedial education of their employees, any pedagogical method that invigorates students' learning and keeps them coming back for more is worth a close look by educators, parents, and business leaders alike.

As President Clinton has stated on numerous occasions, education is our most important bridge to the 21st century. It's one we all have a role in building. In this book you will see that design in education itself constitutes a

powerful bridge, both literally and figuratively. You'll see children building and testing bridges as a means of learning math, science, and social studies. You'll see how design helps teachers bridge different subjects and connect classroom learning with the larger community. Ultimately, whatever the type of design and its curricular context, you'll see that the creative, problem-solving process of design helps both teachers and students achieve their goals.

In closing, I want to thank all those who made this book possible both within and beyond the Arts Endowment and to thank ASCD in particular for recognizing the potential of design to help teachers all across the curriculum. If what you see excites you, as I am sure it will, consider how to integrate these methods into your community's schools, into teacher-training programs, and into school-business partnerships. You will find design a potent catalyst for excellence.

Jane Alexander
Chairman
National Endowment for the Arts

Middle school students design the ideal city of the future for the annual National Engineers Week Future City Competition. Here, the winners show their computer-designed city to President Clinton.

1   Riley, Richard W. (February 18, 1997). Fourth Annual State of American Education Address. Washington, D.C.: U.S. Department of Education, p. 2.

2   Goals 2000: Educate America Act. (1994). Public Law 103-227, signed into law March 31, 1994.

3   *Business Week.* (October 28, 1996). "Educating for the Workplace Through the Arts."

Acknowledgments

Unless you are looking at this book in the middle of a wilderness, you are surrounded by the designed world: the landscapes, buildings, products, and graphic communications that go together to form the world humans have shaped to their own ends—and are constantly in the process of revising and recreating.

Designing is an inherent human capability. We see evidence of humans' creative adaptation to the natural world as far back as archaeologists, anthropologists, and paleontologists can take us. We also see daily, gleeful evidence of design wherever young children are allowed to let their keen curiosity and inventive imaginations engage the world around them.

The act of designing is so multifaceted—encompassing so many synaptic flashes linking mind, eye, and hands—that it is hard to convey its dynamism, much less its pedagogic potential, in the single word "design." Our British colleagues are closer to capturing its Protean character when they talk of the "designerly way of thinking, knowing, and doing."

It is that dynamism and potential that this book attempts to capture and present, to show that design belongs in the curriculum not merely as a noun or verb but as adjective and adverb too. This book also attempts to show that design belongs not only in the art studio and industrial arts (now "technology") classroom but in and among all the disciplines.

As the following pages will reveal, dedicated professionals across the country—teachers, curriculum specialists, and administrators—have seen the potential of design at work. These educators understand that thinking about and "doing" design motivates young people; helps them place what they are learning in a larger context; teaches them how to be both reflective, self-directed learners and collaborative team members; and, best of all, reveals to them that they have both the innate creative capacity and the civic responsibility to manage change in the "built," or designed, environment.

As with any multiyear, multitask project, profound and sincere thanks are due to many people who contributed to and influenced this book:

To Jane Alexander, Chairman of the National Endowment for the Arts, and to the National Council on the Arts for approving the funds for this research project, which was launched in late 1992.

To Mina Berryman, former director of the National Endowment for the Art's Design Program, for first suggesting design in K-12 education as a topic for exploration, and to Samina Quraeshi, her successor, who supported the project to its conclusion.

To the exemplary individuals who generously gave their time and talent to serve on our national advisory com-

mittee for this project. Drawn from the worlds of education and design, they challenged, encouraged, and blessed this effort with confident patience during its many twists and turns. They are:

- **Doug Herbert, Director, Arts in Education, National Endowment for the Arts**

- **Meredith Davis, Head, Graphic Design, North Carolina State University, Raleigh, North Carolina**

- **Gioia Caiola Forman, former principal of Dranesville Elementary School in Herndon, Virginia, and now director, Security and Risk Management, Fairfax County Schools**

- **David Kennedy, Director of Educational Technology, Office of the Superintendent of Public Instruction, Washington State, Olympia**

- **Gary Marx, Senior Associate Executive Director, American Association of School Administrators, Arlington, Virginia**

- **Hazel Robbins, teacher, Shawmont School, Philadelphia, Pennsylvania**

- **Alan R. Sandler, Senior Director, Education Programs, American Architectural Foundation, Washington, D.C.**

- **Julia Shahid, Academic Coordinator, McKinney Independent School District, McKinney, Texas**

To Gertrude (Gerri) Spilka and her colleagues at the OMG Center for Collaborative Learning in Philadelphia, who undertook the initial research for the Design Program, cast the net for

teachers, explored the literature, and placed the testimony of teachers in the broader context of educational theory and practice. The research team she assembled included, at various times, Bernard McMullan, Lisa Nutter, and Mark Fraga.

To Meredith Davis, one of our advisors with experience in both the professional design world and the K-12 classroom, for accepting the challenge of revising the manuscript to elucidate the design methodologies that lie below the surface of the stories told.

And to Ron Brandt, Assistant Executive Director of the Association for Supervision and Curriculum Development, for first seeing the potential of this subject to address the needs of teachers and curriculum specialists in all discipline areas, and to Nancy Modrak, Gary Bloom, Kathie Felix, and René Bahrenfuss at ASCD for shepherding the manuscript through to publication.

Beyond this team, we have been aided by a far-flung network of advocates and practitioners of design-based learning. Hundreds of them nominated teachers for our initial survey. Dozens assisted in identifying sites, resources, and illustrations. Among them I would like to acknowledge the enthusiastic, unstinting support of the following individuals in particular:

PHOTO BY MARC YVES REGIS/
THE HARTFORD COURANT.

- Ken Baynes, Professor of Design Education, University of Loughborough, England

- Charles Burnette, Chair, Industrial Design Department, University of the Arts, Philadelphia, Pennsylvania

- Pamela Carunchio, Director of Education, Foundation for Architecture, Philadelphia, Pennsylvania

- Dorothy Dunn, Director of Education, Cooper Hewitt National Design Museum, New York City, New York

- Ginny Graves, Director, Center for Understanding the Built Environment, Prairie Village, Kansas

- Richard Kimbell, Head, Design Studies Department, and Director, Technology Education Research Unit, Goldsmith's College, University of London, England

- Laura London, Manager, K-12 Education, Autodesk, Inc., Sausalito, California

- Peter Lowe, Executive Director, Worldesign Foundation, Inc., New York

- Doreen Nelson, Professor, School of Education and Integrative Studies, California State Polytechnic University, Pomona, California, and Director, Center for City Building Education, Los Angeles, California

- Kendall Starkweather, Executive Director, International Technology Education Association, Reston, Virginia

- Ronald R. Todd and Patricia Hutchinson, TIES Magazine, College of New Jersey, Trenton, New Jersey

- Anna Sanko, Architecture Resource Center, Connecticut Architecture Foundation, New Haven, Connecticut

- Anna Slafer, former Curator of Education, National Building Museum, and now Executive Director, Renew America, Washington, D.C.

- Anne Taylor, Director, Institute for Environmental Education, School of Architecture and Planning, University of New Mexico, and Director, School Zone Institute, Albuquerque, New Mexico

- Adele Weiler, President, Building Connections, Murray, Utah

Closer to home, I would like to thank several interns and fellows at the National Endowment for the Arts who assisted with various administrative aspects of the project, including Jean Horstman, Rachael Smith, and Sarah Ferguson.

Ultimately my deepest thanks goes out to all the teachers who responded to our call for information and to their many colleagues who take up each day the challenge and excitement of the most noble profession, that of nurturing and educating the next generation of citizens. For as David Perkins has said in *Knowledge as Design*: "A teacher ideally conceived is a designer who helps learners to design themselves."

It is the hope of all those who have contributed to this book that you will find inspiration in its pages for your own work with young people and that this introductory report will also be a catalyst for further research, curriculum development, innovative teacher preparation, and professional development.

—*Peter Hawley, Project Director*

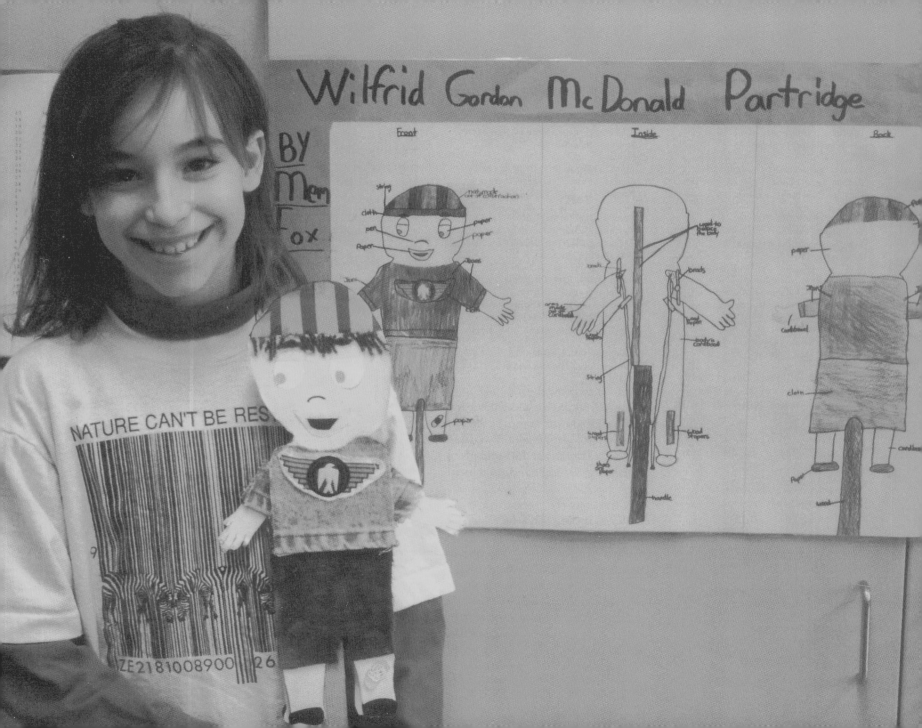

Introduction

In Seattle, Washington, 4th grade students explore relationships between culture and habitat as they design and build Native American housing. Social and environmental studies come alive for them through activities that pose real-life problems, similar to those encountered by residents of the earliest North American communities.

A kindergarten student in West Linn, Oregon, struggles with making a moveable hinge for a puppet she is designing. She knows the performance she wants and works backward through a myriad of possible mechanical solutions that might achieve the gestures she sees in her mind.

In Lowell, Massachusetts, 7th and 8th grade students apply their knowledge in math, science, and environmental studies to critiques of "environmentally unsound packaging." They work in teams to create more effective solutions. As astute consumers of popular culture, they find writing brochures and designing advertising for these products equally engaging.

A high school physics teacher in Aurora, Colorado, reports the success of his "Rube Goldberg Project" in motivating students who normally show no interest in physics. In designing, building, and operating their extraordinary machines, students demonstrate their understanding of physics principles with an enthusiasm their teacher rarely finds in traditional exercises.

And in Canyon Country, California, 6th grade students design and construct a city of the future, acting out the roles of the planning and transportation boards and city council. In addition to learning how civic groups reach decisions, students confront the difficulties of planning urban systems while preserving the quality of community life.

Increasingly, innovative teachers explore with their students the modes of inquiry used by graphic designers, product designers, interior designers, urban planners, landscape architects, and architects.

These students and their teachers employ an approach to learning in which design is an integral part of curriculum and pedagogy. Increasingly, innovative teachers explore with their students the modes of inquiry used by graphic designers, product designers, interior designers, urban planners, landscape architects, and architects. They also examine content related to the everyday artifacts and environments of various cultures, along with processes for making decisions about visual communication, consumer products, and the built (manmade) environment. Finally, these teachers employ active learning experiences that model the cognitive and social problem-solving demands of adult life. Design-based learning offers genuine promise for preparing students to be thinking, informed citizens who can shape progress in the next century. And, for children, design experiences are

intriguing puzzles through which learning comes alive.

The National Endowment for the Arts has long supported the inclusion of design in the K-12 curriculum.[1] In response to growing evidence that design is a powerful tool for transforming curriculum and accommodating the variety of ways in which students learn, the Endowment's Design Program created a special funding category for Design in Education in 1991. Impressed by reports from those who received grants and by anecdotes from classroom teachers and administrators around the country, the Program commissioned a study in 1993 to gain further understanding of how design in the curriculum helps students and teachers achieve national educational objectives and to explore opportunities for expanding the role design can play in students' academic lives. To conduct this research, the Endowment engaged The OMG Center for Collaborative Learning, a public policy research and consulting group based in Philadelphia and Los Angeles. A national advisory panel of K-12 educators, administrators, and design educators guided OMG in its work during 1993 and 1994.

This book presents findings of that research and reveals how the use of design experiences in classrooms provides teachers and students with a learning construct for the next century.

How the Research Was Conducted

THE GOAL OF OMG's research was to show a range of what teachers and students do in design and the promise that design-based teaching and learning hold for education reform, not to identify the best examples of the use of design in U.S. classrooms. Instead of reviewing programs advocating design in schools, OMG's research explored the benefits teachers say design brings to their practice and to their students. Thus, this book summarizes descriptive research that makes qualitative statements regarding current practice and identifies effective models for using design in classrooms. The research team selected an exploratory, hypothesis-generating approach since the practice is in the early stages of adoption and the overall number of educators using design in the classroom is small.

OMG's researchers tapped three primary sources of data:

- a review of literature on the use of design in classrooms,

- a national qualitative survey of teachers currently using design with their students, and

- site visits to 10 schools representing a range in uses of design.

Researchers piloted a survey questionnaire and sent it to 900 teachers nominated by their peers in a Call for Information, which was distributed to educators and design professionals through mailings to schools, professional publications, and electronic networks. The questionnaire probed the way teachers use design: as subject matter in the curriculum, as an experimental means of integrating content across disciplines, and as a thinking process for learning subject matter in many disciplines. It also asked how teachers learn about design and requested samples of their classroom lessons.

More than 160 teachers responded to the questionnaire.[2] The research team analyzed their responses for content and scrutinized lessons for possible case study development. A promising group of responses showed the following:

– a range of ways in which teachers used design,

– varying degrees of integration of design into curriculum, and

– diversity in teachers' understanding of the design process and its use as a learning strategy.

With consideration of these factors and additional attention to diversity in geographic region, grade level, school subject area, and scale of design problems (e.g., graphic, product, architecture, environment), the research team and advisors selected 10 sites to visit.

For each one- to two-day site visit, the research team collected data to supplement the teacher questionnaires and lessons. The team members used two methods.

Direct Observation. The researchers observed classroom and school activities—including design activities and other relevant subject-related work—and the school environment, seeking evidence of the way design-based learning affects or is affected by school culture and physical facilities.

Qualitative Interviews. The researchers conducted qualitative interviews with principals, curriculum coordinators, other school or district administrators, teachers, teachers' aides, students, and parents to gather anecdotal evidence on the role of design in fostering excellent education. The objective was to elicit viewpoints from people with different perspectives on education.

During the observations and interviews, the research team used a template for inquiry to focus the visit and provide consistency from site to site. Researchers asked questions concerning program profile, curriculum, assessment methods, teacher profiles and training, pedagogical strategies, administrative support, facilities, and limitations on the use of design in the classroom.

Following the field work, the research team interviewed college professors of education, state and district curriculum specialists, and educators with experience in other design-based programs for additional information and perspectives.

1 Due to Congressional funding cuts in 1996, separate discipline-based, grant-giving programs at the National Endowment for the Arts were eliminated and reorganized into four broad divisions. One of these, Education and Access, still provides support for pre-K to 12 projects, including those involving design.

2 Unless otherwise noted, comments and project descriptions attributed to individual teachers and students were obtained through questionnaire responses or followup interviews.

How the Book Is Organized

CHAPTER 1 presents a description of the design process, a brief history of the use of design in classrooms in the United States, and a summary of international initiatives.

CHAPTER 2 discusses the learning experiences and outcomes for students who attend design-based classrooms.

CHAPTER 3 focuses on what the use of design in the classroom means for teachers.

CHAPTER 4 summarizes the relationship between design-based approaches and mastery of content in various disciplines.

CHAPTER 5 poses challenges to schools and districts.

CHAPTER 6 discusses conclusions of the research and makes recommendations about teacher education, changes to the support system in schools, and resources to further the understanding of design education and strengthen its use in classrooms across the United States.

APPENDIX A carries information about the consistency of design-based approaches to teaching with goals stated in national reform initiatives.

APPENDIX B lists resource information for teachers and administrators.

APPENDIX C provides a comprehensive listing of the schools that participated in this study.

1

LEARNING
Through Design

The future is not some place we are going to, it is one we are creating. The paths to it are not found, but made, and the making of these pathways changes both the maker and the destination.

UNESCO, "Qualities Required of Education Today to Meet Foreseeable Demands in the Twenty-first Century," 1989, p. 9.

this book addresses the study of design as a subject of investigation and a mode of inquiry that engages a variety of student learning styles and makes direct connections between school subjects and problem solving in daily life. The use of design that is illustrated here applies to children at many grade levels and in a full range of disciplines, not just students involved in precollege design, technical, or art instruction.

Where design itself is the subject of investigation, students focus on the "goodness of fit" among the products of designers' work (visual communication, products, and environments);

the people for whom such products are intended; and the larger physical, social, and cultural contexts of which they are a part. Such design experiences may be active (making something as a solution to a design problem) or reflective (thinking about or commenting on designed objects or environments and their contexts). In cases where designerly modes of inquiry dominate, students may apply design problem-solving strategies to learning about something other than design. In some instances, teachers even may assess what students know about disciplines other than design by asking them to solve a design problem.

The Design Process

ONE PREMISE OF this book is that there is great congruency between the thinking and making processes in which design professionals engage and the demands today's students will likely face as adults. This congruency argues for expanding the application of design methods and the pedagogy of design education to the teaching of many subjects in K-12 classrooms.

It is clear that, to solve the great challenges of the future, the United States needs creative workers and citizens who can overcome the limitations of traditional ways of solving problems, who can invent new strategies that are appropriate to a given situation, and who can adapt to change. To be successful, employees must acquire and comprehend new information and skills at rates previously unimagined. They also must recognize that they are individuals within broader systems and their actions have consequences beyond the immediate time and place. As citizens, they must strengthen the fabric of communities that are more culturally and socially diverse than in previous times. When participating in community decision making, they must honor their own values while respecting the values of others through a well-considered process of choice.

While such demands are likely to characterize the lives of all citizens in the future, they also define the environment for which today's design professionals trained. What serves designers well in a climate of rapid change is their problem-solving process. It is a creative counterpart to the scientific method, and it presumes there is more than one right solution to any problem and many paths to each alternative. Designerly modes of inquiry place no hierarchy among various physical and cognitive skills. For designers, doing is a way of knowing. They are as likely to analyze a problem through models, diagrams, walks through an environment, or sketches as they are through statistics or writing. Designers are fluent in several vehicles of thought (images, words, numbers) and methods of communication, storing and recombining experiences for future use. Their process is iterative, always alerting them to new problems and opportunities.

Nigel Cross, designer and educational researcher in the United Kingdom, states, "The sciences value objectivity, rationality, neutrality, and a concern for the 'truth'.... [T]he humanities value subjectivity, imagination, commitment, and a concern for 'justice'.... [The designerly way of knowing] involves a combination of knowledge and skills from both the sciences and the humanities" (Cross 1983, pp. 221-222).

A 1976 research report from the Royal College of Art in London for the British Secretary of State for Education and Science, titled *Design in General Education,* identifies design as "a third area of education" (Royal College of Art 1976, p. 44). Bruce Archer, former Director of Design Research and the Design Education Unit at the Royal College of Art, cites education in the sciences and in the arts as dominating our social, cultural, and educational systems. In summarizing Archer's report, Cross draws the following conclusions about the nature of design:

- The central concern of design is "the conception and realization of new things."

- It encompasses the appreciation of "the material culture" and the application of "the arts of planning, inventing, making and doing."

- At its core is the language of modeling. It is possible to develop students' aptitudes in this language, equivalent to aptitudes in the language of the sciences (numeracy) and the language of the humanities (literacy).

- Design has its own distinct "things to know, ways of knowing them, and ways of finding out about them" (Cross 1983, pp. 221-222).

While basic sciences rely primarily on the scientific method and the arts on intuition, design is somewhere in between; design activity is based on an approach to acquiring knowledge, skills, and attitudes that responds to the interdisciplinary complexity of life. Science experiments succeed in labs and art responds to personal, subjective criteria, but design products must perform for people. Those engaged in the design process must understand and account for a wide variety of audience and user behaviors in an array of physical, social, and cultural contexts.

There is growing attention to the notion that a design education produces problem solvers whose thinking skills are in marked contrast to students schooled in other disciplines. In *How Designers Think* (Lawson 1990), Bryan Lawson recounts his study of advanced students majoring in science and architecture. Each group tackled the same problem requiring the arrangement of colored blocks in order to satisfy certain known and unknown rules. Lawson found contrasts in the problem-solving strategies of the two groups. The scientists tried to discern the rules from a systematic exploration of all possible combinations, while the architects proposed possible rules and eliminated them through experimentation with various combinations. In other words, scientists were problem oriented, while architects were solution oriented; scientists favored analysis, while architects tended to synthesize. Lawson repeated the study with younger students at the beginning of their science and design educations. The two groups showed no significant differences in their problem-solving strategies. He concluded that the differences exhibited by more advanced students must be the result of their education (Lawson 1979).

If society values the thinking and problem-solving behaviors exhibited by designers, there must be greater investment in developing these skills in all students across all subject areas. One way to accomplish this is to involve students directly in the design process. The design process, although often modified to fit specific circumstances and individuals, generally includes these aspects:

- identifying and defining problems,

- gathering and analyzing information,

- determining performance criteria for successful solutions,

- generating alternative solutions and building prototypes,

- evaluating and selecting appropriate solutions,

- implementing choices, and

- evaluating outcomes.

Although practice is shifting, most classroom procedures favor teacher-driven assignments, criteria for excellence, and assessments. Design experiences, on the other hand,

Two additional common uses of the term "design" appear in discussions of design-based teaching and learning.

The first encompasses precollege or technical education intended to prepare students for either professional practice or employment as technical support in fields such as graphic design, illustration, product design, fashion design, interior design, or architecture. In this instance, design is used in the classroom to give college-bound students a jump-start on career education or to provide students who are not going to college with experiences that qualify them for future employment in technical service industries.

The second covers experiences in the aesthetic arrangement of abstract two- and three-dimensional form, commonly referred to as study of the "elements and principles of design." Such activities and discussions usually form the basis of introductory art classes and focus on self-expression or technique through painting, sculpture, printmaking, and other fine arts media. While design disciplines share with the fine arts a concern for aesthetic principles, the design disciplines focus primarily on shaping communication, objects, and environments as responses to human problems.

Figure 1.1

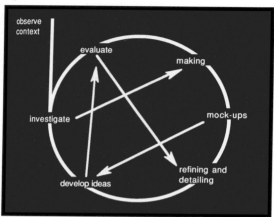

Design Process

Figure 1.2

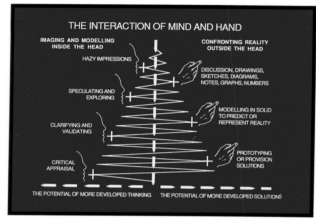

The Interaction of Mind and Hand

encourage students to think critically and weigh options through participation in problem solving. In generating alternative solutions to problems, the design process urges iterative work in which students test and refine multiple solutions. Modeling and diagramming share equal respect with quantitative means of communication and evaluation, often better revealing the true relationships among ideas and allowing students with differing learning preferences to work within their individual strengths. While *analysis* has a role to play in this process, the ultimate goal is *synthesis* and determining a solution that addresses the breadth of performance criteria set forth by the problem.

Any discussion of the design process runs the risk of failing to capture its active nature. Investigating as an activity

is typically assessed through a passive research report; the process is measured through the product. Schools have a tendency to convert active processes into linear series of passive products. British education professor and expert on educational assessment Richard Kimbell sought an appropriate diagram to express the dynamic aspects of the design process to his Assessment Performance Unit, a group charged with evaluating the national design and technology curriculum in the United Kingdom (Kimbell, Stables, Wheeler, Wosniak, and Kelly 1991). Kimbell's interacting design loop in Figure 1.1 captures the divergent and cyclical nature of the design process.

Kimbell goes one step further in describing the design process by modeling the interaction between mind and

hand (Figure 1.2) to show why and how students using the design process choose to do things, rather than what they do. Figure 1.2 also illustrates how design activities develop fluency of thought operations (i.e., thinking in both images and words) in ways that solely reflective activities do not. Kimbell describes student involvement in the design process as "thought in action," which challenges the traditional schism between thinking and doing found in many school curricula (Kimbell et al. 1991, p. 20).

The work of Dennie Palmer Wolf reinforces the value of the design process as a model for teaching and learning. Wolf talks of the need to teach and assess "enterprise" rather than "school subjects"; to engage students in learning activities that model the integrated, synthetic problem solving demanded

Three Decades of Design in U.S. Classrooms

of adults in their work; and to build meaningful connections among skills and knowledge that too often remain the purview of discrete academic disciplines (Wolf 1994).

Nigel Cross explains the unique role design experiences play in helping children make connections across disciplines and to life: "Designing is a process of pattern synthesis, rather than pattern recognition. The solution is not simply lying there among the data, like the dog among the spots in the well known perceptual puzzle; it has to be actively constructed by the designer's own efforts" (Cross 1983, p. 224).

Designers recognize that their cognitive skills and use of nonlinear processes are highly relevant to the complex nature of contemporary work and life. Many of these design professionals, as well as researchers who recognize the relevance of design to learning, have a fervent interest in contributing to new teaching practices that respond to natural differences in the ways students learn best and promote students' mastery of a full repertoire of problem-solving skills. For the first time in recent history, these interests align with the common goals of educational reform. (For further discussion of design and education reform, see Appendix A.)

TEACHERS USING design in today's K-12 classrooms build on a 30-year legacy established by designers and design educators. Past programs brought designers into classrooms, trained teachers to develop and conduct their own design activities, established professional networks that supported teacher interest in design, and published innovative curricula and learning materials that broadened the influence of design on teaching practices.

Developed in the 1960s to support greater coherence between education and changes in industry, early design programs were generally at the secondary school level and encouraged practice in the technical skills necessary for work in design professions that served an expanding economy. These programs were largely preprofessional and technical, as defined in the margin note on page 3.

Other programs in the 1960s and early 1970s professed a more activist agenda, however, helping students understand and participate in decisions about the built (or manmade) environment. Designers of these programs aimed at developing informed citizens who demand and respect well-designed products and buildings, who make discriminating judgments about visual communication, and who function as full participants in the design of their

Designing and building a prototype observation deck.

5

communities. Some piggy-backed on the growth in environmental education programs that followed major environmental legislation in the 1970s.

For example, architects Richard Saul Wurman and Alan Levy, under the title Group for Environmental Education (GEE), developed a curriculum for Philadelphia middle schools that involved students in activities about the city and its design. A curriculum from the Cranbrook Academy of Art, Problem Solving in the Man-Made Environment, targeted 7th grade social studies students in Michigan middle schools with information that encouraged intelligent consumer choices about the design of communication, products, and places. Like many programs, these efforts were short-lived and their publications are out of print.

Other programs that emerged during this period continue, gaining national attention and outreach. Among them are Ginny Graves' Center for Understanding the Built Environment, Doreen Nelson's Center for City Building Education, the Salvadori Education Center on the Built Environment, Anne Taylor's School Zone Institute, and Sharon Sutton's Urban Network. While these programs focus primarily on architecture and community planning issues, they have a broader purpose to educate young citizens who exercise

greater social and political control over decisions throughout their everyday lives.

Heritage education is another established point of entry to the study of design. Concern over the destruction of important architectural landmarks resulted in school programs aimed at instilling in children a respect for the past and their built legacy. Heritage education programs focus "primarily on older and historic manmade structures and environments, promoting their use in the curriculum as visual resources for teaching knowledge and skills, as artifacts for the study of a continuum of cultures, and as real and actual places that students of all ages can experience, study, and evaluate firsthand" (National Council for Preservation Education 1987). While experiences in which students actually construct buildings and environments enrich their understanding of their built legacy, heritage education more often includes replication of historic designs than new problem solving.

More recently, the availability of low-cost computers and a shift in the nation's workforce from product-based to service-based activity has provided the impetus for transforming traditional "industrial arts" instruction into "technology education." Software companies see opportunities to create

new, long-term users for their products and provide resources to schools at low cost. This sponsorship expands schools' potential to integrate technology at all levels of the curriculum and in a variety of disciplines. Subjects that traditionally had little visual content gain a design dimension through software that produces charts and graphs, models structures, and opens up opportunities for typographic experimentation.

Another stream of technology education finds its roots in engineering and design. While the emphasis in these programs is on designing technology itself, rather than on the use of computer software, proponents of this approach still find confusion among educators. The International Technology Education Association (ITEA) defines technology education as "the study of the application of knowledge, creativity, and resources to solve problems and extend human potential" (Bottrill, 1995, p. 41). Yet there persists a lack of recognition by many educators that a special kind of thinking is required to invent technology that solves a human problem—and that this thinking is quite different from the cognitive skills necessary to use technology designed by someone else or to design machines that don't address the social context of their use. Adequately preparing students to explore and invent new relationships

Designing is

what humans do.

between man and machine remains a challenge. Among the program developers wrestling with this problem are Project UPDATE and TIES Magazine, based at the College of New Jersey in Trenton.

Continuing unrest with schools whose teaching practices frequently do not reflect current research about how children learn also spawns interest among K-12 educators in using design-based activities to teach other subjects and to connect curricula with students' lives outside school. In these schools, teachers employ more open-ended, active learning experiences that foster creativity and expand the role for design from object of inquiry to include method of inquiry.

Two programs that use active learning and the design process to help students understand content in a variety of disciplines are the Design-Based Education Program, developed by industrial design educator Charles Burnette and offered through the Art and Museum Education Department at the University of the Arts in Philadelphia, and the Education through Design Program, developed by Meredith Davis and Robin Moore at the School of Design at North Carolina State University. In both programs, as in Doreen Nelson's City Building Education, the focus is on educating teachers in design and

creativity rather than relying on designers-in-residence or prepackaged curricula. In some cases, these programs represent collaboration between colleges of design and education.

Professional design associations and institutions support this development in K-12 design-based education. The largest initiative is the Learning by Design Program developed by the American Architectural Foundation of the American Institute of Architects.

In addition to publishing design lesson plans in teacher magazines, multimedia classroom kits on the White House and U.S. Capitol, and a Sourcebook of exemplary learning activities, this program also has stimulated grass-roots collaborations between teachers and designers through small grants to chapters of the American Institute for Architects. Some local efforts, such as the Foundation for Architecture in Philadelphia and the Chicago Architec-

Experimenting with linear design elements, students construct a toothpick tower.

[Through design projects,] my students gain a sense of control over their lives because they believe they can solve any problem that confronts them throughout their lives. The students also have more confidence in making decisions and in presenting their ideas to others. The presentation and critique process helps the students to practice and gain confidence in these skills.

PAUL DEVINE, 9-12 technology teacher, Wilmington, DE

ture Foundation, also have developed extensive school programs involving workshops, team teaching, curriculum materials, and student competitions.

The American Planning Association encourages its members to work with teachers, publishes a quarterly newsletter devoted to K-12 education, and highlights design-related curriculum materials in its publications catalogs. The Worldesign Foundation, an outgrowth of the Industrial Designers Society of America, recently adopted K-12 education in design as one of three priorities for its national and international efforts, along with advocating greater awareness of the critical links between design, environmental quality, and job creation.

Design-related museums have been particularly active in supporting both formal and informal design education programs for young people. The National Building Museum in Washington, D.C., established its DesignWise program in the 1980s to provide workshops for teachers and students and to develop curriculum materials. Similarly, the education department of the Cooper-Hewitt National Design Museum in New York City serves as a resource for teachers nationwide, sponsors summer institutes for teachers, and offers a wide array of museum- and neighborhood-based design education

programs for students in the metropolitan area.

The National Endowment for the Arts also supported design education through its Architecture-in-the-Schools initiative in the 1980s and seed grants for curriculum development projects. Some state arts councils continue to support designer residencies and the Endowment provides matching grants for K-12 projects through its Education and Access Division.

Despite this level of innovation during the last 30 years, the use of design activities in U.S. schools remains an isolated practice that has its strongest support at the level of the individual teacher. Documentation of teacher work is spotty and many educators labor with little more than moral support for their efforts at district and state levels. The individual initiative required to establish and sustain these programs within a somewhat indifferent administrative culture leaves little time and few resources for the systematic and rigorous assessment that would present convincing evidence for broader adoption.

Many of the programs mentioned above focus study around the interests of their initial developers and supporters. For example, architecture and heritage education focus on issues in the built environment and are typically the lenses through which many programs develop. Technology education, supported by software developers, frequently focuses on the acquisition of technical skills and the use of computers. Graphic and industrial design programs are less common and are often geographically centered near their developers. This focus on special interests results in a rather fragmented effort to promote the use of design in U.S. classrooms and little collaboration among program developers. Many successful programs in schools disappear when their curriculum developers or teachers move on to other venues because school administrators make no provisions for systemwide teacher training and institutional adoption of practices.

During the past few decades there has been a lively exchange of information between many proponents of design education in the United States and their counterparts abroad. This includes sharing journals, studies, and curriculum materials; attending international conferences; and visiting one another's schools.

DESIGN APPEARS in educational policy and practice around the globe. Sometimes an explicit component of a national curriculum, design more often is implicit in the emphasis placed on problem solving and the use of references from the designed world.

While the use of design in education is not the focus of any comprehensive documentation, studies of international trends in science, technology, and environmental education reveal growing acknowledgment by educators of the need to change instruction in ways

... ways that integrate design problem solving as a natural component of learning

Perhaps the greatest influences on design-based teaching in the United States come from the United Kingdom, where design and technology are subjects in the national curriculum. Many examinations in British schools require students to design and make objects. To the right is a motorbike design created by a 15-year-old student who then made a model of the bike (below).

reflection that result in curricular innovation, student teamwork, increased connection among disciplines, application of learning to contexts outside of school, and teacher modeling of the behaviors they seek to instill in students.

Learning from the United Kingdom

Perhaps the greatest influences on design-based teaching in the United States come from the United Kingdom, where design and technology are subjects in the national curriculum. Building on a long history of training in the crafts and increased interest in science, math, and technology spawned during the post-Sputnik era, the United Kingdom began efforts to introduce technology in schools as early as the 1970s. Funded by the central government's Schools Council, Project Technology made a strong case for a national technology curriculum, while the Design and Craft Education Project sought to revise existing subjects with a new emphasis on

that integrate design problem solving as a natural component of learning.

A variety of economic, environmental, and social imperatives fuel the international adoption of design-based strategies. In industrial and developing nations alike, public and private sector leaders recognize that young people must graduate from compulsory education systems with strong, flexible skills if they are to compete successfully for jobs in the global marketplace. The answer seems to lie in giving priority to activities that build up students' practical capability in tackling realistically complex problems with social and

human dimensions. Burgeoning populations, finite natural resources, and unsustainable patterns of consumption, manufacturing, building, and transportation are wake-up calls to educators to revisit the underlying assumptions of school curricula (Black and Atkin 1996, p. 90).

Within the context of these pressures, certain principles of pedagogical reform gain widespread support. Emerging educational practices show remarkable similarity with the tenets of design-based teaching and learning: student-centered classrooms, self-directed learning, teacher collaboration and design and technology. At the same time, the government's Department of Education and Science funded research on Design in General Education at the Royal College of Art in London. Led by Bruce Archer and Ken Baynes, this project analyzed the characteristics of designing in an attempt to describe a category of human endeavor analogous to the sciences and the humanities.

By the late 1970s, design and technology was a recognized part of the curriculum in the United Kingdom and in 1981 the Department of Education initiated a series of studies to develop and evaluate techniques for assessing student performance in the subject. The most comprehensive of these was developed under the direction of Richard Kimbell at the University of London from 1985 to 1991.

In 1988, Parliament passed the Education Reform Act, calling for a national curriculum of required subjects for all students ages five to 16. Informed by the advocacy of the Design Council (a quasi-governmental body established to promote better design in British industry, raise public awareness of design's value, and promote design education in schools), the National Curriculum Council recommended technology as one of 10 foundation subjects in the compulsory national curriculum, encompassing both Design

and Technology and Information Technology. Parliament accepted this recommendation and adopted the curriculum for England and Wales in 1990. A 1995 revision made Information Technology a separate subject and modified some of the content and assessment requirements in design (Eggleston 1996, p. 43).

Passage of the national curriculum stimulated an impressive array of curriculum materials, teacher training, demonstration programs, and research, much of which informs the work of design education proponents in the United States. At all grade levels, the British national curriculum calls for students to design and make objects, systems, and environments in response to the needs and opportunities they identify. Teachers encourage pupils to look for problems to solve through design in five broad contexts: home, school, recreation, community, and business and industry, progressing from familiar to unfamiliar settings in successive grades.

American educators have maintained a lively dialogue with British educators, attended their conferences, and subscribed to their publications. Leading British theorists and practitioners also consult in this country. Ken Baynes of Loughborough University; Eileen Adams, at Southbank University; Richard Kimbell at Goldsmith's College, University of London; and Peter Sellwood at Westminster College, Oxford, have all had a hand in shaping the thinking of American curriculum innovators.

British teachers encourage pupils to look for problems to solve through design in five broad contexts: home, school, recreation, community, and business and industry. Here, an 8-year-old student has created a design for protective clothing.

Students evaluate the integrity of their design by adding weights to a bridge spanning two tables.

Design and Technology for All Students

The United Kingdom is not alone in its concern for all students' command of design and technology. In its 1996 study of science, mathematics, and technology, the Organization for Economic Cooperation and Development (OECD) notes that many countries that once separated students into vocational-technical tracks at a relatively young age now see the need to provide all students with a grounding in technological competency (Black and Atkin 1996, p. 54). Examples from around the world show that progress is being made in achieving this goal.

In 1993, the Australian Education Council, with the support of education authorities at the state, territorial, and Commonwealth levels, recommended national curriculum frameworks and achievement targets in eight "key learning areas," including technology and studies of the environment and society.

In technology, the Council emphasized that students should learn through "designing, making, and appraising" at every grade level and in every content area, including information, materials, and systems. The Council expects students to "investigate issues and needs, devise proposals and alternatives, produce products and processes, and evaluate consequences and outcomes." Students should "take responsibility for designs, decisions, actions and assessments; trial their proposals and plans; take risks when exploring new ideas and practices; and be open-minded and show respect for individual differences when responding to technological challenges" (Cowley and Williamson 1995, pp. 2-4).

This ambitious agenda for Australian children was tested at the Lauderdale Primary School in the seaside community of Hobart, Tasmania, in 1994-1995. Projects ranged from the design of shelter to studies of the movement of snails on

design perspectives and activities helped children understand the relationship between economic forces, the ways in which people make their living, and the resulting changes to the surrounding landscape.

Responding to Environmental Concerns

While environmental education in many parts of the world is little more than nature appreciation, the United Nations' International Environmental Education Program (IEEP) believes that the 1992 Earth Summit in Rio de Janeiro brought about a "major shift in international thinking" with its emphasis on teaching for sustainable development. Recognition that such instruction must integrate issues of environment, population, and social/economic development is apparent in a number of programs around the world. Content in these programs addresses not only the degradation of ecosystems but the ways in which products, packaging, buildings, and cities can be made more "earth-friendly." (United Nations Educational, Cultural, and Scientific Organization, June 1995, p. 2).

A 1994 study undertaken for the U.S. Agency for International Development finds that redefinitions of environmental

various surfaces. The OECD observed hands-on student-centered learning, collegial interaction among faculty, and strong modeling by teachers of the same behaviors they expect from students. Teachers at every grade level made frequent use of design briefs that "involved the students in reflective processes; whether they were being asked to write a story or design a room, they have to consider the purpose of the work and the materials available, and design, make, and continually appraise the match between their product and the required outcome" (Cowley and Williamson 1995, p. 28).

Also in 1993, both the Netherlands and Scotland adopted technology as a required subject for students, ages 12-15 and 5-14 respectively. Dutch teachers emphasize "functional knowledge" and research and communication skills (Franssen et al. 1995, p. 5). In Scotland, where technology is part of Environmental Studies, OECD researchers observed that "opportunities were made for students to work on tasks which were practical, which involved creativity, which encouraged children to think within the framework of the design process and which were sustained by genuine interest" (Kormylo and Frame 1995, p. 12). In particular, they found that programs in Latin America and the Caribbean emphasize reciprocal relationships between individuals, society, and the natural world. In Costa Rica, 7th through 9th grade students learn how to protect watersheds through more sustainable forms of human settlement, while in Jamaica, 9th grade social studies students weigh the impact of industry and other human activity on the environment (Arias-LaForgia 1994, pp. 36, 53).

Similarly, a study of 13 nations in Asia and the Pacific by the Tokyo-based National Institute for Educational Research (NIER) identifies a trend in which nature study and the management of natural resources are no longer seen as the only issues of concern in environmental education. Instead, topics related to the quality of life (such as housing, sanitation, transportation, and recreation) appear as important components of curriculum (National Institute for Educational Research [NIER]

1993, p. 3). In Malaysia, Singapore, and Thailand, environmental problem solving permeates a variety of school subjects. In the Philippines, where the national curriculum emphasizes "totality of coverage" including "natural, man-made, technological, and social aspects of the environment," teacher training prepares educators to tackle these issues (NIER 1993, p. 90).

Rapid industrialization in Korea and Japan prompted increased curricular emphasis on environmental issues. Korean students at all levels investigate the human, social, and natural dimensions of the environment and develop their own solutions to creating "a pleasant way to live." In Japan, the national curriculum calls for comprehensive attention to environmental topics in primary and secondary schools, with particular emphasis on developing students' problem-solving skills and ability to respond actively to social change. Environmental issues and hands-on

experiences span the full range of school disciplines (NIER 1993, p. 68).

In Europe, many countries are revamping curricula to emphasize links between the built and natural environments. The OECD documents changing national policies and innovative school projects include two reports: *Environment, Schools, and Active Learning* (Organization for Economic Cooperation and Development [OECD] 1991) and *Environmental Learning for the 21st Century* (OECD 1995).

Belgium recently revised its curriculum to encourage project-based environmental education, emphasizing problem solving, action-oriented forms of learning, and a focus on the local community. Interdisciplinary activities range from the analysis of city housing and traffic problems to comprehensive environmental studies of entire regions. Students present their findings in public presentations, newspaper and radio reports, postcards, and videos.

In Austrian schools, students designed and established two parks, developed more environmentally friendly means for packaging products, and crafted a development plan for a small wine-growing village. German students converted an abandoned school into a nature center, while on the coast of Italy, 12-year-olds engaged in a one year study of the economic and ecological impact of a new port facility.

OECD reports that these initiatives demonstrate benefits of using the community beyond the school as a textbook in which the nature of problems demands interdisciplinary understanding: "... experience shows that students can work with surprising success in the local community, using it both as a source of local knowledge of their environment, as well as a field for developing their skills in problem solving, entrepreneurship ... and informing adults about local environmental issues" (OECD 1995, p. 99).

At the same time, OECD sees "a serious deficiency everywhere [in] the lack of integration of economics, politics, sociology, and other social sciences in understanding environmental issues ... In order for a new 'environmental education paradigm' to develop, there is the need for the creation of a fresh knowledge base that can master the complexity of the interdisciplinary nature of environmental issues" (OECD 1995, p. 88). The authors point to the holistic design-based problem-solving approaches of highlighted schools as guideposts to the future.

Children in Sendai, Japan, explore tension and compression in structures using chopsticks, rubber bands, and paper.

U.S. educators have responded to overtures for exchange from Japanese educators. Here, Doreen Nelson from California State Polytechnic University leads a city building education workshop for students, teachers, and government officials at Tohoku Koka Joho College in Sendai, Japan.

Americans Reach Out

Since 1987, when a traveling exhibit called the One Hundred Languages of Children first introduced Americans to Reggio Emilia's innovative early childhood education programs, numerous educators from the U.S. have traveled to Italy to visit the design-rich infant-toddler centers and preprimary schools established by Loris Malaguzzi. Countless more have discovered these schools through the book of the same name and subsequent conferences.

At the heart of the schools' success is the creative, collaborative, project-oriented work that children and teachers undertake together. Unique features introduced by Malaguzzi are the atelier or studio and the full-time position of atelierista. Placed in a prominent, visible location in each school, the studio is a workshop filled with all types of tools, construction materials, and art supplies. Though trained in the visual arts, the atelierista does not "teach" art, but instead serves as a helpful guide to children and teachers alike in the proper and possible uses of materials. He or she also helps teachers document and understand the children's creative and cognitive processes (Edwards, Gandini, and Forman 1993).

Recently, U.S. educators have responded to overtures for exchange from Japanese educators. Anne Taylor, Director of the School Zone Institute and professor of architecture at the University of New Mexico, invited Japanese educators to attend the 1992 International Summit on Children and Architecture held at the university. Through exchanges organized by Taylor, U.S. advocates and practitioners of design-based education have lectured at major Japanese universities and provided teacher training in Tokyo, Sendai, Nigata, and other cities. Contingents of Japanese teachers also observed design-based practices in this country.

Japan's Ministry of Education recently initiated research on the benefits of a design approach to general education at the University of Tokyo School of Education. Responding to a ministry call for more environmental education at all levels, the Japanese translated Taylor's Architecture and Children curriculum into their language and now use regional and vernacular curriculum supplements to it. Under the sponsorship of the Architectural Institute of Japan, the American Institute of Architects, and the City of Matsubase, Doreen Nelson and her colleagues in the Departments of Education, Environmental Design, and Instructional Technology at California State Polytechnic University (Pomona) are developing a Web site that will enable children and their teachers in both countries to engage in joint city building projects on the Internet.

Formal acknowledgment of design as important content, context, and methodology for learning varies greatly from one country to the next. Yet, is clear that at both individual and institutional levels, curiosity and support for its use are increasing. As the world moves into the 21st century, it remains to be seen whether educators in the United States and other countries can overcome the disciplinary, institutional, and cultural hurdles to greater use of design in the classroom.

References

Arias-La Forgia, A. (1994). *Environmental Education in the School Systems of Latin America and the Caribbean, Working Papers, No. 4*. Washington, D.C.: Academy for Educational Development for the Education and Human Resources Division, Bureau for Latin America and the Caribbean, U.S. Agency for International Development.

Black, P. and Atkin, J.M., eds. (1996). *Changing the Subject: Innovations in Science, Mathematics, and Technology Education*. New York: Routledge, with the Organization for Economic Cooperation and Development (OECD), Paris, France.

Bottrill, P. (1995). *Designing and Learning in the Elementary School*. Reston, Virginia: International Technology Education Association.

Cowley, T. and Williamson, J. (1995). *OECD Report on Science, Mathematics and Technology in Education (SMTE) Project*. Launceston, Tasmania: University of Tasmania, School of Education.

Cross, N. (October 1983). "Designerly Ways of Knowing." *Design Studies* 3, 4: 221-224.

Edwards, C., Gandini, L., and Forman, G., eds. (1993). *The Hundred Languages of Children: The Reggio Emilia Approach to Early Childhood Education*. Norwood, New Jersey: Ablex Publishing Corporation.

Eggleston, J. (1996). *Teaching Design and Technology, 2nd edition*. Philadelphia, Pennsylvania: Open University Press.

Franssen, H.A.M., Eijkelhof, H.M.C., Houtveen, A.A.M., Duijmelinck, H.A.J.P. (1995). *Technology as a School Subject in Junior Secondary School in the Netherlands*. Utrecht, the Netherlands: University of Utrecht, Department of Education.

Kimbell, R., Stables, K., Wheeler, T., Wosniak, A., Kelly, V. (1991). *The Assessment of Performance in Design and Technology*. London, England: School Examinations and Assessment Council.

Kormylo, P. and Frame, J. (1995). *A Report on Technology in Case Study Primary Schools in Scotland*. Edinburgh, Scotland: Scottish Office Education Department.

Lawson, B. (1979). "Cognitive Strategies in Architectural Design." *Ergonomics* 22, 1: 59-68.

Lawson, B. (1990). *How Designers Think: The Design Process Demystified,* 2nd edition. Oxford, England: Butterworth-Architecture.

National Council for Preservation Education. (1987). *A Heritage at Risk: A Report on Heritage Education K-12*. Burlington, Vermont: University of Vermont Historic Preservation Program.

National Institute for Educational Research. (1993). *Environmental Education and Teacher Education in Asia and the Pacific*. Tokyo, Japan: NIER.

Organization for Economic Cooperation and Development. (1991). *Environment, Schools, and Active Learning*. Paris, France: OECD.

Organization for Economic Cooperation and Development. (1995). *Environmental Learning for the 21st Century*. Paris, France: OECD.

Royal College of Art. (1976). *Design in General Education, Part One, Summary of Findings and Recommendations*. London, England: Royal College of Art.

United Nations Educational, Cultural, and Scientific Organization. (June 1995). *Connect, the UNESCO-UNEP Environmental Education Newsletter*, p. 2. Paris, France: UNESCO.

Wolf, D. (July 1994). Presentation at Skidmore College, Saratoga Springs, New York.

The design process, although often modified to fit specific circumstances and individuals, generally includes these aspects:

- identifying and defining problems,

- gathering and analyzing information,

- determining performance criteria for successful solutions,

- generating alternative solutions and building prototypes,

- evaluating and selecting appropriate solutions,

- implementing choices, and

- evaluating outcomes.

2 LIFELONG *Learning*

Using design concepts in my classroom has increased the students' problem-solving capabilities. It encourages synectic thinking, which permits students to see similarities between dissimilar things.

WENDY CONNOR, 6-8 art, Jackson Hole Middle School, Jackson, WY

U.S. leaders generally agree that adults who are successful have flexible thinking skills and the facility to acquire and apply new knowledge and skills to unfamiliar tasks and settings. In a time of rapid change, it is this ability to adapt learning and develop new problem-solving strategies that determines success.

Most K-12 curricula reflect a time when it was possible to learn a well-defined body of knowledge that society agreed was critical to adult life and work. But today, given our rapidly changing world, learning strategies that emphasize storing facts in memory are inadequate. When faced with this sort of education, students' motivation to learn understandably wanes because

they see no immediate relevance to their own lives of either the facts or the learning methods they are taught. Unless changes are made, we are in danger of producing a generation of adults who lack the basic thinking skills for survival in the next century.

Schools that do teach thinking processes frequently emphasize linear "recipes" that may or may not match the divergent nature of contemporary problems and students' own preferences for learning. In many cases, the process becomes another fact to learn, a procedure without context or applied value in the student's world. The task for educators is to reinvigorate learning and to model the integrated, dynamic processes we expect students to use as

responsible, successful adults.

The research for this book suggests that using design experiences in the classroom accomplishes that task. Teachers report that their primary motivation for using design is to help students acquire the necessary competencies to meet new challenges throughout their lives. At the top of teachers' reasons for making design a critical part of their curriculum and teaching strategies are:

- **enhancing flexible thinking skills,**
- **promoting self-directed learning and assessment,**
- **developing students' interpersonal and communication skills, and**
- **cultivating responsible citizens.**

19

Enhancing Flexible Thinking Skills

TO ENHANCE STUDENTS' thinking skills, educators must instill in students a process for creative problem solving that transcends individual assignments, illustrates how learning applies to students' everyday lives, builds relationships across traditional school subjects, and increases students' comfort with the uncertainty that characterizes many problems. In addition, assessment must become a matter of students' internal accountability for the achievement of high standards.

Strengthening Creative Problem Solving

Developing and strengthening creative problem-solving skills is a more difficult challenge than it appears. Education researchers define maintenance learning as the acquisition of fixed outlooks, methods, and rules for dealing with known and recurring situations. Innovative learning, on the other hand, questions assumptions, seeks new perspectives, and facilitates transfer to new problems and settings. While curriculum can easily challenge students to solve problems, it must work very hard to teach processes and ways of thinking that transcend assigned tasks (Nickerson, Perkins, and Smith 1985).

Research evidence suggests that the design process is an innovative model for strengthening students' creative

problem-solving skills. Because the design process concerns itself with "that which does not yet exist," it encourages learning behaviors that prepare students for an environment of change.

Willamette Primary School in West Linn, Oregon, is explicit in its use of the design process. Teachers employ design in curriculum development and their own study of education; students discuss the process and use it to solve a variety of problems across disciplines. Classes always document their process in notebooks, on bulletin boards, or in classroom and hall displays. For Willamette, the design process consists of these iterative problem-solving steps and questions:

- **Define the context and the problem.** What do you want to know, and what do you already know about the problem?

- **Plan and conduct research.** How will you conduct the research? Will you observe, read, interview, sketch, or build models?

- **Generate criteria for a successful problem solution.** What is the rubric or set of criteria against which you will measure performance?

- **Generate solutions.** What are the alternative solutions?

- **Implement.** How can you realize and test the best solutions?

- **Evaluate.** What were the criteria addressed by the solutions? What needs modification to better meet the performance criteria?

- **Reflect on the process.** What was done throughout the process? What was effective? What could have been improved?

Scott Wavra, a 4th and 5th grade teacher at Willamette, illustrates this process as he describes the efforts of his students in designing a home for their pet snake.

My class needed to design and construct a cage for an eight-foot python, who could only stay in the classroom if the class was able to house him. The children asked questions about the needs of snakes and then studied reference books and collected information about large snakes. Cage criteria were listed by the group. Children sketched at least three designs {for the cage}, each incorporating the learning from their research. Then the class pooled the different ideas and developed a rubric of critical design elements.

Teams of children discussed options and created a group plan. They were taught how to draw their plans to scale orthographically, and then they brainstormed the types of materials construction would require. The teams made a corresponding list of prototype materials {for testing their ideas}. They calculated the viewing area (area) and the room the snake would need to move (volume). Each team developed a budget, constructed scale prototypes, and tested them with a smaller garden snake. Each group prepared and gave a persuasive speech about the most effective elements of their design.

The whole class used that information to develop the best cage with all of the best elements of each presentation, and put together one last blueprint to request construction funds from the school administration. Once those plans passed inspection, the children built the cage, complete with heating and lighting.

This is powerful learning that replicates what society demands of successful adults. It begins with a highly motivating problem: keeping the live snake in the classroom. Students analyze this problem and set the appropriate criteria against which their solutions will be judged. The assignment drives their search for facts; they acquire knowledge within a context and make active use of it. Resources and their uses are self-determined and, therefore, highly motivating.

In addition, the problem demands that they move back and forth through visual/spatial, linguistic, and mathematical thought and communication. Students link concepts from science, mathematics, construction technology, economics, and art. They weigh each choice against a preferred outcome, and

they act as contributing members of a team in making decisions. This design-based learning experience teaches students a problem-solving process they can adapt to many situations. They learn about reptiles, building, and habitat in ways that dramatically increase the likelihood of retention. Best of all, they leave the classroom feeling successful about learning and anticipating the next day's events.

The research team noted numerous instances in which teachers and students reflected on their problem-solving processes. At such times, teachers made conscious attempts to comment on the process and remind students of other circumstances in which the process might be helpful. As at Willamette, many schools use journals in which students record their thoughts about design experiences. Dolores Patton, a 3rd and 4th grade teacher using Doreen Nelson's City Building

The Pull Toy
I made a Blueprint. I got
some tsring and some brads.
Then I got my paper, and my
scissors. I cut out my shapes.
Then I started fiddling with my
stuff until I got the right design.
And now I pull The string and
The ears move.

Education at Open Charter Magnet School in Los Angeles, California, asks students to write about their methods, diagram or illustrate them, and post their drawings on the class "history wall." This serves as an enlarged journal record of the problem-solving process. The wall constantly changes with each addition, modeling the dynamic process of creative thought.

As David Perkins notes, "Design in education with reflection [on process] offers opportunity for students to take the learning from one problem and extend it further. It creates the chance for teachers to move students from the immediate concrete problem to general processes of problem solving that can be applied elsewhere" (Brandt 1986).

At Locust Valley Intermediate School in Locust Valley, New York, teacher Wendy Fein confirms Perkins' view of the design process through her work with students: "The design process promotes organizational skills and creativity — two seemingly opposite concepts that must coexist in a truly effective learning environment. Creativity without some form of organization can result in chaos…. Rapid advances in technology and information demand that students acquire the organized, step-by-step design process that will permit [them] to grow into productive and effective adults, able to succeed in a rapidly changing world…. [The design process] is easily transferred to problem solving in any discipline."

Applying Learning to Students' Everyday Lives

As John Dewey noted in 1910, a critical failing of school is that it was conceived as a separate place where lessons were learned and certain habits formed (Dewey 1910). Today, this remains true for many children. Many educators assert that students leave school before graduation in part because they cannot see how education benefits them in life. Abstract concepts and principles learned in school frequently exhibit little relevance to the environment in which children live, play, and work. The problems teachers ask students to solve share little with the problems they f ace in daily life and over which they exercise some control.

Whether focusing on everyday problems in immediately observable settings or projecting problems into the future, using design in the classroom builds bridges between school and life. Rather than beginning with abstractions, design activities demand that students *derive* concepts and principles from real encounters with their world. They learn the unfamiliar by finding it in or comparing it to what they already know. As William Perry, an 8th grade art teacher at Banksville Gifted Center in Pittsburgh, Pennsylvania, observes, "Any time I can demonstrate for my students the necessity for, and applica-

tion of, learning, thinking, and doing, I gain credibility. Recognizing the importance of design [in this process] moves the classroom from the hypothetical to the real world — and to their worlds."

The research team identified numerous examples of students engaged in exploration of their own environment. Ruth Hiebert, a 5th and 6th grade teacher at Soledad Canyon Elementary School in Canyon Country, California, builds her 5th grade curriculum around City Building Education and a set of personal questions that allow students to make connections among concepts at scales starting with the individual: Who am I? Who am I in the classroom? Who am I in the small group? Who am I in the community? Who am I in the United States? Who am I on planet earth?

Students work in small groups to draw floor plans and build models of the classroom. They explore the importance of furniture arrangement and lighting to create the type of human interactions they expect in the classroom. Later in the year, the class takes field trips to study different systems in the city: sewer and power plants, parks, and bus depots. Discussion centers on how these systems are necessary to maintain life in the city and how each is related to the next in a web of interdependency. Students then design and build their own mini-cities.

At Locust Valley Intermediate School, Wendy Fein uses a project on urban planning to teach students how their community works.

Students use census information to construct a town that complies with the needs of the population and their view of a better way of life.... Students must reach consensus on what the town will be zoned for, where the zones will be located, what physical features exist and must be built around, what variances are acceptable.... Sixth graders, as part of this project, construct maps that include nodes, landmarks, and major and minor paths from their homes to school.

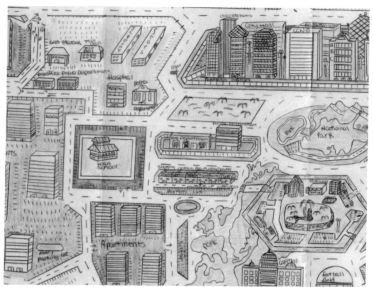

Because the products of design problem solving are everywhere, there is enormous opportunity to engage the full range of children's interests with problems that relate directly to their own lives while simultaneously supporting the teaching of required curricula. William Suess, a technology education teacher at Cape Henlopen High School in Lewes, Delaware, asks students to design a simple way of preventing inebriated teenagers from starting their cars on prom night. The task meets the teacher's objectives for having students understand technology and drafting while encouraging them to examine their own attitudes and behavior.

At the same time, design activities make it possible to explore ideas through another person's eyes. In Barbara Van Wicklin's 3rd and 4th grade classes in rural Allegany County, New York, stu-

dents grapple with the difficulties that poor design sometimes creates for people with disabilities. As an exercise, they redesign the lunchroom ketchup packet to make it usable by a wide range of people. In doing so, they learn how decisions about the physical environment sometimes impede people's ability to perform simple activities. These students also realize that they too might one day experience difficulty with products and the designed environment, if only through the natural processes of aging.

As Martin and Jacqueline Brooks observe, a constructivist approach builds from students' own questions and knowledge and contrasts to learning approaches that assume knowledge is gained by copying it directly from the external world and a fixed curriculum (1993, pp. 15-20). In a design approach to learning, issues and concepts motivate questions and transcend the arbitrary divisions of content in textbooks and among school subjects.

Building Relationships Across Traditional School Subjects

Current reform initiatives and standards in the various school subjects share concern for students' ability to think in terms of systems and across disciplines. An understanding of "connectedness" is critical to work and responsible decision making in the future.

Design author and methodologist J. Christopher Jones describes a hierarchy of problems in society (see Figure 2.1). At the lower end of the hierarchy are problems at the component and product levels. These are usually the preoccupation of less developed societies (Jones 1970, p. 30).

Many of our contemporary challenges in postindustrial society, however, reside at the systems and community levels of Jones's hierarchy. For example, the decay of American cities, environmental

Figure 2.1

> **J. Christopher Jones'
> Hierarchy of Problems**
>
> ▲
>
> **COMMUNITY**
> (formed by interrelated systems, such as transportation, communication, housing, natural environment, etc.)
>
> ▲
>
> **SYSTEMS**
> (formed by interrelated products, such as cars, roads, airplanes, and maps in the transportation system)
>
> ▲
>
> **PRODUCTS**
>
> ▲
>
> **COMPONENTS**

Source: J. Christopher Jones, *Design Methods*, p. 30 (New York: John Wiley & Sons Ltd., 1970).

With Nelson, the teaching team generates alternative activities to teach students about the concept of "changing size."

- Find four ways to make an equation bigger.

- Find examples of "bigger" in science fiction movies.

- Make a sound bigger.

- Make an object bigger.

- Make a composition bigger.

- Study the parallels and contrasts between local, state, and federal government.

pollution, and inadequate nutrition for all children result from complex webs of interrelated problems. Current curricula and teaching practices, however, usually foster skills and center knowledge around the component and product problem-solving levels. By focusing tasks that are discipline-specific or that do not situate the study of objects and ideas within larger contexts, schools educate a workforce and citizens who cannot meet challenges at the upper levels of Jones's problem hierarchy.

Design activities and the use of the design process in teaching subject matter other than design force students to confront how their subject of study is part of a larger system. For example, a student design for a city park must take into account the environmental impact of its location, the political system by which the community makes decisions, the species of plant life that will thrive within its boundaries, the range of physical capabilities and interests of its users, and so on. Even a simple poster design is part of a communication system that connects to cultural, social, and physical contexts through its use.

Interest in interdisciplinary and cross-disciplinary learning intensifies as educators help students to transfer basic problem-solving strategies to diverse and complex situations. To do this, schools must teach basic competencies in core subject areas as well as show relationships among these disciplines, thus heightening their relevancy (Jacobs 1989). Many educators also argue that interdisciplinary studies have as their primary objective the development of higher-order critical thinking skills: comparing, contrasting, synthesizing, structuring, and innovating.

Design is inherently interdisciplinary and encourages systems thinking. It combines concepts and thinking skills found in both art and science, and it concerns itself with social, cultural, and physical contexts. Likewise, the most successful uses of design in the classroom are interdisciplinary. While there is a tendency to think of design activities as the purview of the art or industrial arts class—due largely to definitions of design education that focus on visual aesthetics or preprofessional training—design has relevance

25

across the curriculum. As the python cage example illustrates, richly defined design problems force students to make connections among seemingly disparate facts and subject areas. Integration among subjects is seamless in design projects, unlike some learning activities where teachers force connections to meet curriculum mandates for inter-disciplinary instruction.

The research for this book revealed many examples in which the design process helped children articulate relationships and concepts across one or several disciplines. As Dolores Patton and Leslie Barclay demonstrate in their work with City Building Education at Los Angeles Open Charter Magnet School, students move freely across disciplines when given the opportunity. A project on "change" asks students to compare a drawing, sentence, and sound event that use the same concept of change. For example, a child makes his drawing "split" by dividing it into two pieces. He then makes sound "split" by putting silence in the middle.

Patton describes her work across disciplines and how it contributes to her effectiveness as a teacher.

Design gives me a means to connect my teaching and build more meaningful path-ways from one topic to another.... I find that it is much easier to connect seemingly incongruous topics. {The use of design} is even more powerful than thematic instruc-tion because it weaves one theme to another. When we {study} everyday objects, we can discuss how a teapot is organized so it can pour effectively. When we discuss organiza-tion, we can compare city water systems to the teapot. The children follow this simile readily, excitedly adding modifications to clarify the example.

The research revealed another exam-ple of helping students develop skills across disciplines at Willis Intermediate School in Delaware, Ohio. Science teacher Teresa Bettac uses design activities to link science and business in a unit she calls "To Be a Scientist." Students research the work and times of a famous scien-tist. They review scientific literature and interpret the scientist's discoveries through different media. Students then write and design a logo and brochure for a science-related company. They also must apply for a job at one of the "new" firms, using their scientist's credentials and persona. They complete a resume and job application and interview for the job. Through this project, students frame what they know about science in a business portfolio. Communication to others about what they learn about sci-entists and their work plays a primary role in the activity.

At Tippecanoe Elementary School for the Humanities in Milwaukee, Wisconsin, design serves as a thematic unit for the whole school. Teachers integrate subjects to contrast, compare, and develop students' understanding of how disciplinary boundaries overlap. Each year the school sets a different theme for activities in all grades. A program implementer assists classroom teachers and the art teacher with pro-ject-based activities. One theme was "Experiences and Places: More than Meets the Eye." As program imple-menter Steven Shaw says, "We are interested in helping students develop an understanding of how the built environment is affected by different times in history, people, science and technology, and the constraints of structures and math-ematical relationships." Students create alphabet books based on shapes in the built environment, visit the Milwaukee Public Museum to examine scale models of buildings, work on maps in a study of abstract symbols that represent the environment, and compare how different rooms in a house have changed over time.

While the design process is inherently interdisciplinary or cross-disciplinary in nature, classroom design activities do not necessarily dictate shared instruction among teachers of different disciplines. There are many examples in the research study in which teachers find design activities effective in placing discipline-specific subject matter in broader contexts that children understand. Chapter 4 illustrates how design activities support the work of specific disciplines.

Increasing Student Comfort with Uncertainty

The problems of today's world are messy and ill-defined. A primary challenge to tomorrow's leaders will be managing the uncertainties that characterize contemporary life. Design deals with these forces through methods of both divergent and convergent thinking and through attitudes that tolerate ambiguity and suspend judgment in the early stages of problem solving.

Through design problems, children learn to think laterally, generating many alternatives rather than progressing through a linear process to one right answer. They experiment through trial and error in an effort to truly understand the dimensions of the problem, as well as the range of potential solutions. In doing so, students explore alternatives that attempt to reconcile competing values by weighing the different outcomes that result from ranking some aspects of the problem above others. Because design focuses on moving conditions from the "existing to the preferred" (Simon 1969), students learn to imagine

the consequences of possible choices. This type of activity is in contrast to most school assignments that require students to execute a linear sequence of tasks in response to a problem for which the outcome is usually known.

"Making sense" of the problem appears in the work of a 5th grade student at Epiphany School in Seattle, Washington, who has the task of constructing a "yurt," a portable domed tent used by nomadic Mongols. The project is teacher Deirdre McCrary's effort to illustrate the physical properties and limitations of materials within the context of another environment and another culture's housing needs, as well as the value of trial and error in determining what a problem is really about.

students **learn to imagine** the consequences of possible choices

Promoting Self-Directed Learning and Assessment

The student is to determine its actual appearance, its size, and the materials of which it is made in building a model. After failing at several attempts to create a form with toothpicks, dowels, tree branches, glue, and paper, {one} child walks away from his work. Several minutes later, he returns and announces, "The branches told me how to do it!" He realizes the limits of the toothpicks and the potential of the tree branches in achieving the size and form of something he imagines as a yurt: "The toothpicks could only bend so far without breaking, but I could get the tree sticks to bend much further. I realized the only way I could get the effect I wanted was with the branches."

Students who are comfortable with uncertainties in the early stages of problem solving are more likely to take calculated risks and to view failure as a way to learn rather than as defeat. They also learn to suspend judgment until they view facts and circumstances from many vantage points. While this is a useful strategy for solving individual problems, it is also a strategy for life. As adults, these students will have to accept challenges for which there are no prescribed methodologies, invent new paradigms, and sustain interest in their work despite intermittent setbacks.

IF INTEREST AND skill in lifelong learning are key objectives of education, it is imperative that schools help students take responsibility for their own learning. Child-centered, constructivist approaches to learning provide practice in *posing* questions as well as *solving* problems. Students learn to challenge assumptions and the ranking of priorities intrinsic to problem definitions. They ask themselves what values are implicit in the structure of the problem and how broad a context they must address.

In an exercise to design clothing for people with physical disabilities, high school students meet and observe their "clients." The students ask questions regarding movement and how people dress. Through this process they set performance criteria against which they and their users will measure the success of solutions. In doing so, students realize they cannot accommodate all needs equally well; they must assign higher value to some criteria and, where possible, reconcile conflicting demands. Students also learn a new perspective in thinking about people with disabilities. They see that the environment and everyday objects "handicap" people, not their disabilities.

This example contrasts with more traditional curricular structures in which the problem statements students

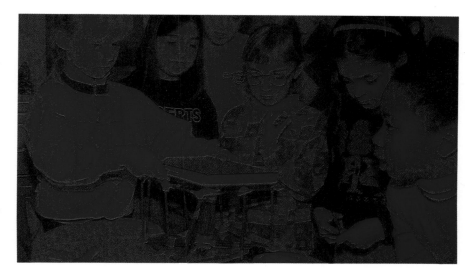

receive from teachers are more prescriptive in their procedural expectations and criteria for success. As David Perkins asserts, typical math problems faced by most children today are proofs of knowledge already known: "Although you can calculate the height from which you have to drop an ice cube to vaporize it, or the leverage required to budge the Empire State Building, who cares?" (Perkins 1986, p. 97). The teacher frames the question and knows the answer; the student's task is to find out what the teacher already knows and values. There is no self-determination, no active context in these types of problems and, as researchers testify, low student motivation to solve them.

Good design problems share common characteristics in what they ask of children. Although they may be tightly defined, often by the teacher, their solutions are not predictable; each student ranks the importance of individual variables differently, resulting in different problem-solving methods and solutions to the same problem statement. Problems that require students to reconcile conflicting priorities (e.g., cup designs that are elegant but disposable, chair designs that are sturdy but portable) open opportunities for rich discussion about why certain criteria

are more important than others. When the solution to the problem has no observable precedent, such as a paper bridge that can support a brick, motivation is high and students stretch their understanding of basic principles in an attempt to discover a solution.

Design problems also engage students in what design author and methodologist J. Christopher Jones calls "glass box" thinking: stepping outside of the process to watch oneself solve a problem (Jones 1970, pp. 49-50). Because no future design problem will be exactly the same as the one they are now solving, students learn to focus on their process as the true content of activities. This self-reflection and self-evaluation helps students learn from their failures and build on their successes. Karen Miller, a 2nd and 3rd grade teacher at Willamette Primary School, reinforces the value of self-reflection.

In an exercise developed for the national assessment in the arts, four cups are examined to identify design priorities (stability, heat retention, disposability, etc.) and a fifth cup is designed that combines apparently competing priorities (stable and stackable, elegant and disposable, etc.).

I meet individually with the children to discuss their reflections on learning, and check for understanding across a broad range of skills.... The class and I create a rubric that acts as a standard that guides our work. We consider the purpose and characteristics of work we admire. The children evaluate themselves at the conclusion of a project, not only on the product, but in what areas they have grown and what they have learned that might help them in a future project. We have a working journal in which we record thinking and progress throughout the project.

Sharing Responsibility for Assessment

As educators across the country develop more effective, large-scale strategies for determining what students know and are able to do, the issue of authentic assessment at the levels of classrooms and individual students remains a high priority for teachers, students, and their parents. Dennie Palmer Wolf's Performance Assessment Collaboratives with Education (PACE) at Harvard pioneers the effort to develop assessment strategies that authentically model the performances expected of children in their adult lives. Wolf believes concern for measuring and reporting achievement data to external audiences drives

most traditional assessments, and that these approaches do not help students develop their own internal systems of accountability. Nor does traditional testing nurture the student's desire to achieve high standards or provide the means to establish a personal sense of excellence. Instead, such assessment encourages a temporary acquisition of facts as proof of mastery against criteria the student does not necessarily value (Wolf 1992).

New assessments, such as those endorsed by Wolf, value "formative reflection," ongoing feedback throughout a project that reshapes the processes and final products of learning. Formative reflection allows teachers to engage students and their peers in interactive assessment and mirrors the tradition of "progress critiques" found in college-level design classes. Assessment of this sort supports powerful learning and builds a school culture of high standards.

The fit between design and these new assessment strategies is strong. Design problems present opportunities for project-based situated learning in which products are the focus of periodic critiques of student process. Embedded within the design process is iterative work through which students evaluate, adjust, and redirect behavior in response to feedback on emerging products or design solutions. Performance criteria,

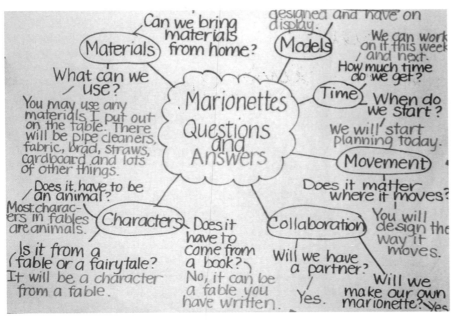

Marionettes Questions and Answers

Materials — Can we bring materials from home?

What can we use? You may use any materials I put out on the table. There will be pipe cleaners, fabric, brad, straws, cardboard and lots of other things.

Models — designed and have on display. We can work on it this week and next. How much time do we get?

Time — When do we start? We will start planning today.

Does it have to be an animal? Most characters in fables are animals.

Characters — Is it from a fable or a fairytale? It will be a character from a fable.

Does it have to come from a book? No, it can be a fable you have written.

Movement — Does it matter where it moves? You will design the way it moves.

Collaboration — Will we have a partner? Yes. Will we make our own marionette? Yes.

Making animal marionettes sparks students' creativity and questions. The Research Web helps them get started.

stated at the front end of the design process, provide students with the rubrics against which they will measure success. Because students often participate in the development and articulation of these criteria, they value their achievement over what appear to be the arbitrarily set rubrics in traditional testing. Because there are many appropriate solutions to the same design problem, design-based learning and assessment strategies tolerate a range of excellent performances. Unlike traditional testing, design projects accommodate the variety of learning styles in any classroom by allowing students to demonstrate mastery and thinking processes in the manner most comfortable to them.

This match between the design process and authentic assessment also signals that a design activity itself may be an appropriate way to evaluate what students know and are able to do in subject areas other than design. For example, modeling the human digestive system from parts found in the hardware store can tell a teacher much about students' understanding of the human body. In this instance, the design task requires that students know how the relevant parts of the human body work and match the digestive operation to the apparent function of hardware. The design task is simply a way to determine to what degree students' knowledge of physiology is operational.

Site visits and teacher questionnaires for this study suggest that, where design strategies are part of a well-considered comprehensive program, students tend to develop internal accountability and take responsibility for achieving high standards of performance. In these schools, assessment is an ongoing shared responsibility among teachers and students, a natural part of the communication climate in the classroom.

Even very young children can set the standard for and assess excellence in their work. Susan Dunn and Rob Larson, authors of *Design Technology: Children's Engineering,* maintain "children may also generate rubrics, or open sets of criteria through extracting successful qualities of models. Children use examples of work and talk about features which are 'good'. Using the children's language, the teacher lists [their] ideas…. In developing such a list, a rubric is not artificially imposed;

31

it comes from the children's experiences and perceptions. Children can use the rubric to develop, reflect on, and modify their designs" (Dunn and Larson 1990, p. 71).

The research team observed student accountability for powerful learning at Willamette Primary School, where several teachers commented on assessment. Kim Turner, a 2nd and 3rd grade teacher, notes, "The children and I set the standard for quality work for each project by creating a rubric. The work is regularly assessed by the children and myself together, and parents are invited to offer comments too. In this way, children learn to view

evaluation as integral to learning and something that should continue at home. It is not just a reporting exercise." Turner's colleague, Janice Leonetti, adds, "I notice a rising spiral of quality in the work the children have produced over time. As a group we talk about good solutions and good approaches as part of the learning process. The best work from one project raises the standard for all in the next project."

Scott Wavra, who teaches 4th and 5th grade students at Willamette Primary School, talks about the use of portfolios in assessment, "We gather student portfolios over the six years children are with us. The portfolios

are evidence of the children's growth over time and their best thinking at any particular time. I look for qualities in the way a child works: asking questions, gathering information, organizing and presenting information, as well as developing an understanding of the social and scientific concepts that provide the framework for a particular study. I am always concerned that upon completing a study, a child has the will to continue learning to take on new and greater challenges."

Teresa Bettac, science teacher at Willis Intermediate School in Delaware, Ohio, also uses portfolios as one means of assessment. "All of my students keep a portfolio of work for the three years I have them in advanced science class. They have an opportunity to add to their portfolio at any time. They are also able to see the variety of designs they have created in three years. Plus they are able to see development and improvement in their [understanding of] design and science concepts."

There is also evidence that traditional testing practices keep certain students from demonstrating competency in core disciplinary content and skills. At Smoky Hill High School in Aurora, Colorado, physics teacher David Pinkerton notes that the use of design in the classroom lets "students traditionally shut out from higher

Developing Students' Interpersonal and Communication Skills

grades in science" demonstrate understanding through projects rather than written tests. Pinkerton indicates, however, that student performance on standardized tests did not change when he adopted a design approach to teaching. In addition to tests and design projects, he now conducts interviews with students as a form of assessment. Through these interviews he learns that the use of design in his classroom results in "an increase in process skills, creativity, intuition, design skills, troubleshooting, physical manipulation, and thinking on your feet. In other words, content has not been sacrificed for process, yet more process is being learned…. My techniques foster long-term memory of ideas and concepts. I have had enough returning college students tell me this that I know it's true."

The research team witnessed students' shared and self-evaluation as one of the strongest characteristics of site-visit schools. By involving students in the development of meaningful performance criteria, the design process embeds assessment in the normal activity of solving problems. By providing opportunities for reflection and self-direction of effort, design activities help students learn to trust their own ability to master concepts and skills.

INTERPERSONAL SKILLS are critical to success at all ages and in all endeavors. These skills are important in the workplace, but they are no less important in the civic realm. Likewise, the ability to construct or interpret meaning in all types of communication is critical to success in today's environment of information overload. The research revealed numerous examples in which design activities fostered competency in collaborative team work and a variety of communication skills.

Fostering Collaborative Teamwork

When educators noted the disparity between the fact that most adults work with teams of people while students often work alone, they began experiments with student learning groups and teams. A decade of research at the Johns Hopkins Team Learning Project suggests that team learning consistently results in accelerated achievement and better retention for all students (Slavin 1986).

Collaborative learning also develops interpersonal skills. In other research, Johnson, Johnson, and Holubec (1994) describe the elements of cooperative learning as:

– clearly perceived interdependence among students;

– considerable face-to-face interaction;

– clearly perceived individual accountability and personal responsibility to achieve group goals;

– frequent use of relevant interpersonal and small-group skills; and

– frequent and regular group processing of current functioning to improve future effectiveness.

The cross-disciplinary and multiphase nature of many design problems provides rich opportunity to nurture students' collaborative skills across all these dimensions. Many teachers report that the complexity of design problems allows children with different skills and different "ways of knowing" to contribute at different moments in the process and to present a variety of viewpoints throughout the process.

For example, at Willamette Primary School, Merilee Bales' 4th and 5th grade children worked together on a class-designed coral reef as they studied habitats.

The goal is to create a life-size coral reef in the classroom. The class divides into subgroups to tackle various aspects of the problem. In each subgroup students assign roles, such as recorder, resource person, and process observer. Later, the same children divide reef-design tasks according to their interests and expertise. All of the children gather information in writing about the elements of the coral reef. When it comes to the actual construction of the reef, with sharks, starfish, blowfish, and coral, several students are fast learners of wire and papier mache techniques. They teach their classmates, and with these students as experts, skills spread quickly through the class. Many children act as assistants when the groups need an extra pair of hands.

While Bales reports that she begins by helping the children divide tasks, they soon assume this responsibility themselves. Similarly, she notes that early in the year students need her help in resolving group conflicts, but as the year and involvement in design activities progress, children become negotiators and resolve their own disagreements.

Smoky Hill High School physics teacher David Pinkerton also has students form their own design teams, but he makes suggestions about recruiting others with skills that complement those of the people already on the team. Manette Gampel, a science teacher at Dyker Heights Intermediate School in Brooklyn, New York, comments on her students' understanding of group design work: "I may have an excellent idea for a bridge, but I am not a skilled artist. My friend, on the other hand, is a skilled artist who can take my idea and translate it into an actual design on paper. The final product is a reflection of both our talents."

Throughout our study, we saw evidence that participation in design activities helps to build student confidence and a sense of control over their own learning. Students are "learning partners" with their teachers, as well as with their classmates. Dolores Patton reports that the use of design in her classroom transforms her students.

Some of the most important changes in the students are their increased independence, poise, and confidence. The children approach new situations more confidently, looking for similarities with other projects. They ask questions more readily, often startling adults with their insights during field trips and presentations. I also notice more camaraderie with my students. Since design is a topic that can readily be observed by all, we enjoy sharing observations concerning designs we encounter. My comments about chair design are compared to the observations of children, who are entirely different "chair clients." There is a warmth and freedom in the classroom when comments by student and teacher are valued more equally.

Teachers also recount that design activities enable students to provide constructive feedback to their classmates.

Teachers remark that many students develop critical language skills and learn to be thoughtful in giving and receiving criticism. One 2nd grade student said, "You learn that someone's tough opinion about your project has nothing to do with you; even though what they say may hurt at first, it's really only about your work. It's not about you as a person."

At Willamette Primary School, teachers encourage students to think about and articulate the processes they use while engaged in design and technology activities. Students record their own problem-solving steps in journals and portfolios, describe them in conversations with the teacher and peer-group teams, and learn to evaluate their own work and that of others. As important, students learn how to document and describe their design process for those beyond the classroom: other school children, teachers, parents, and visitors.

Whether placed in the classroom, in the hallway, or in another public space at the school, student project displays do not just show the final products achieved, but carefully delineate the steps in the process, the questions raised along the way, and the alternatives considered. The children also capture work-in-progress in still photographs or on video, enabling

them to produce narrated slide-tapes and videos summarizing their learning process for parents or community partners.

The school's founding principal, Jane Stickney, encouraged such analysis and documentation inside and outside the classroom as a means of reinforcing student ability and ease in reflection, providing "teaching opportunities" throughout the school building, and communicating the values and outcomes of design-based pedagogy to parents and other community supporters. Evidence of the children's comfort with such reflection proved both personally gratifying and professionally validating: "In the school's second year, when I began to see older students gathered together in the hallway—even during their free time—examining the project displays of younger students and discussing among themselves the processes used, I knew the school was going to be a success."

Stickney is not alone in her observations about student interest in the work of other children. As part of the LEGO City project at Dranesville Elementary School in Herndon, Virginia, in which each class constructs different components of an ideal city from LEGO pieces, a student "community planning team" builds skills in working with multi-age teams of

One result [of education] is that students graduate without knowing how to think in whole systems, how to find connections, how to ask big questions, and how to separate the trivial from the important. Now more than ever, however, we need people who think broadly and understand systems, connections, patterns, and root causes.

DAVID ORR, *Earth in Mind*, 1995

the **best**
work is not always the
result of one person's
efforts.

children. Representatives from all grade levels consider the whole town and review proposals from each student construction team (e.g., housing, roads, parks) before giving approval for work to begin. The planning team prepares and distributes weekly advisories and decisions to each class as they refine the overall community plan. This example mirrors the complexity of adult tasks in organizations of various kinds.

Clearly, design activities make the point for children that the best work is not always the result of one person's efforts. Through the design process, students gain insight into the value of teamwork and how to organize themselves for effective problem solving.

Developing a Variety of Communication Skills

The ability to communicate to others in a variety of appropriate ways becomes increasingly important in an era of rapidly changing technology. A culture that shifted from predominantly oral communication to the use of printed texts now often chooses the image (preferably a moving image) over the word. We process increasing amounts of information visually, via television,

illustrations, and diagrams in newspapers, textbooks, reports, computer multimedia, and photography. In previous eras, illustrations elaborated on text. Today, text explains what we cannot surmise from the illustration. It is not uncommon for magazine readers to go no deeper than perusal of headlines, captions, and photographs to determine the content of an article.

Just as some traditional curricula discourage the use of multiple intelligences, they also handicap students' development of fluency in various forms of communication and interpretation. By relying primarily on verbal and mathematical forms of communication for serious study in today's classrooms, schools fail to develop students as discriminating readers of visual form and as communicators in the languages of their times. Ironically, as budget cuts threaten art education—one of the few disciplines that encourages visual thinking and communication—the demand to be critical authors and readers of visual forms is expanding at an alarming rate.

The design process encourages liberal use of many forms of communication. Well-developed communication cultures exist in all of the site visit schools and their descriptions recur in teacher surveys. At Willis Intermediate School, a 7th grade science class makes

three-dimensional models to demonstrate how water can power vehicles. Teacher Teresa Bettac also encourages students to diagram as a way of understanding science concepts: "Trying to teach science today without using the many elements of design would be boring, but also would make an already complex subject even much harder to understand. Design strategies help students understand difficult concepts. For example, a student who has diagrammed the external and internal parts of a grasshopper has a much better understanding of where to locate and find the organs when they complete a dissection."

The research team also found examples in which computers enhance students' visualization and presentation skills. At Dranesville Elementary School and San Jose Middle School in Novato, California, students work with a variety of Autodesk graphics software programs to present research findings. Dranesville students studying insects design and animate an imaginary bug in an appropriate habitat. Will Fowler's San Jose students create multimedia presentations that reference David Macaulay's *Castle* video in their storyboards and computer animations about life in the Middle Ages. Some students create "fly-throughs" of their three-dimensional computer models. In other lessons, Fowler uses Macaulay's *Roman City* video as the basis for a social studies lesson.

Equally important in today's world is the ability to make coherent, persuasive oral presentations. Design activities require students to summarize findings, pose questions, articulate rationales, and critique solutions publicly at various stages of the design process. Numerous teachers responding to the research survey commented on the degree to which design activities make children active "presenters" in their classrooms and confident in explaining their activities to adults.

Learning to be discriminating "readers" of form is also possible through design-based strategies. Rubie Blount, a 9th grade English teacher at Hillside High School in Durham, North Carolina, asks her students to make a "behavior map" of the room, noting the room's good points and where it does not support the work of the class. They then talk about the changes in their own behavior that might result from several alternate arrangements.

Blount says, "After analyzing the messages conveyed by the simple arrangement of chairs in a room in our discussion of 'the rhetoric of rooms,' I vowed to test the contention that my classroom design sets me up as an unreachable monarch." After the class rearranges the room according to one of their proposed designs, Blount remarks, "They love sitting in the semicircle!... I can easily make eye contact with each student in the class. Mutiny ensued when I tried to get them to move their desks back in the neat little rows [at the end of the day]" (Davis and Moore 1992, p. 23).

Another example of "reading the environment" is evident in architecture professor Paul Tesar's visit to Kathy Allen's 7th grade social studies class in Warren County, North Carolina. Tesar's project is an adaptation of an activity designed by educator Juan Pablo Bonta that asks student teams to design well-known building types (e.g., house, church, bank, city hall) using simple geometric blocks. Students then guess the building type expressed by each team's design. The activity follows with a discussion of the language of built form and an analysis of the physical elements that lead to right and wrong readings of building type. The class also discusses the cultural origins of certain structural arrangements and offers ideas about how another culture might express the same function through different forms and materials (Davis and Moore 1992, pp. 51-52).

Dolores Patton also describes activities in which children "read" the environment. On a visit to the Los Angeles City Hall to watch the proceedings of a city council meeting, Patton asks students to study the design of the building. "How does its design connote power and security? What is the importance of the rotunda as an intersection? How is symbolism used to honor the history of the city?" Patton's students return to the classroom to design a new city hall for their model city of the future with a better understanding of the language of built form and its role in projecting the values of the city.

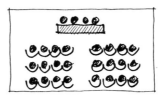

Some teachers ask their students to explore alternate room arrangements to show that the room plan can affect behavior and communication. Above, an illustration titled "The Rhetoric of Rooms" from *Education Through Design* by Meredith Davis and Robin Moore.

Cultivating Responsible Citizens

THE RESEARCH study revealed many examples in which design activities help students at all levels learn about the processes that control local decision-making and how to play active roles in their own communities.

In some schools, students actively experience the political and social processes of their communities. For example, in a suburb of metropolitan Kansas City, Kansas, 3rd grade students at the Stilwell Elementary School toured their neighborhood while studying the history of their town. On their tour, they admired a round barn constructed in 1912. When these students later learned of a demolition plan to make

room for new development, they organized to save the barn. The students made persuasive t-shirts, conducted walking tours for town residents, and produced a slide show on the barn, which they presented to the City Council. As a result of their efforts, their Kansas City suburb still has a round barn (Graves 1997, p. 117).

At Willamette Primary School, students learned that they can affect decisions about the school environment. Working with technical assistants from the community, students designed and built a green space within the school. Former principal Jane Stickney describes the experience: "The idea for the green space came from children who wanted to create a garden on the school site. The children established processes for finding answers to their questions. They worked in teams with community mentors [environmental specialists, engineers, and educators] to collect information [about the site], and to design and build the green space.... They built a sense of belonging and purpose. And most of all, they made something for the community that started off as only an idea."

While these examples illustrate the empowering nature of active design, other teachers report similar outcomes from role playing the type of decision making that takes place in our society.

One of the more successful examples is the student simulation of city government in Doreen Nelson's City Building Education program. Students study terrain, demographics, and land-use decisions. They evaluate transportation and circulation systems within their city, as well as structures for commerce, government, housing, and recreation. As a decisionmaking body for the planning of a future city, the student-formed government coordinates development and oversees the daily activities of production. Students assume the roles of mayor, council members, and commissioners for departments such as education, parks, libraries, housing, utilities, and transportation. Nelson (1984) says:

As it begins to function, the class experiences its own authority or lack of it; the obligations of the group, the nature and function of leadership; and the conflicts arising between the needs of the community and the freedom of the individual. Failures in the first organization lead to more research and reorganization.... Because organizational structures cannot function without procedures, lessons are required in the basics of conducting meetings, following an agenda, delegating work to committees and other skills that are essential for a group to function.

At Willamette Primary School, design activities helped students learn that they can affect decisions about the school environment. After working to design and build a school green space, one student commissioner wrote about environmental needs.

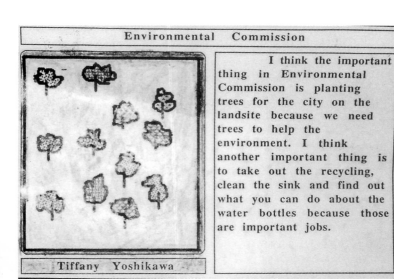

Environmental Commission

I think the important thing in Environmental Commission is planting trees for the city on the landsite because we need trees to help the environment. I think another important thing is to take out the recycling, clean the sink and find out what you can do about the water bottles because those are important jobs.

Tiffany Yoshikawa

Design activities also encourage contact with people in the community and provide insight into how groups make design decisions. At Beaver Acres School in Beaverton, Oregon, 2nd, 3rd, and 4th graders working with teacher Pete Ellenzweig prepare for their building and city design projects in a variety of ways. They conduct book research and, when feasible, site visits and interviews with elected officials, residents, and other adults. They study the immediate neighborhood and nearby Portland, taking walking tours, sketching buildings, and examining various aspects of the urban environment. Reading, listening, and direct observation inform their own city planning projects, including the layout of residential and commercial areas and the design of individual facilities such as the zoo, train station, and football stadium.

It is evident from these examples that design activities empower students to make decisions, modeling the responsibilities of adult citizens. Through design, students learn the consequences of such decisions and prepare to be active participants in shaping their physical, social, and cultural environments.

References

Brandt, R. (May 1986). "On Creativity and Thinking Skills: A Conversation with David Perkins." *Educational Leadership* 43, 8: 13-18.

Brooks, J.G. and Brooks, M.G. (1993). *In Search of Understanding: The Case for Constructivist Classrooms.* Alexandria, Virginia: Association for Supervision and Curriculum Development.

Davis, M. and Moore, R. (1992). *Education Through Design: The Middle School Curriculum.* Raleigh, North Carolina: North Carolina State University.

Dewey, J. (1910). *My Pedagogic Creed.* Chicago, Illinois: A. Flanagan Company.

Dunn, S. and Larson, R. (1990). *Design Technology: Children's Engineering.* Bristol, Pennsylvania: The Falmer Press.

Graves, G. (1997). *Walk around the Block.* Prairie Village, Kansas: Center for Understanding the Built Environment.

Jacobs, H.H. (1989). *Interdisciplinary Curriculum: Design and Implementation.* Alexandria, Virginia: Association for Supervision and Curriculum Development.

Johnson, D., Johnson, R., and Holubec, E.J. (1994). *The New Circles of Learning: Cooperation in the Classroom and School.* Alexandria, Virginia: Association for Supervision and Curriculum Development.

Jones, J.C. (1970). *Design Methods.* New York: John Wiley and Sons.

Nelson, D. (1984). *Transformations: Process and Theory.* Los Angeles, California: City Building Education.

Nickerson, R., Perkins, D., and Smith, E. (1985). *The Teaching of Thinking.* Hillsdale, New Jersey: Erlbaum Associates.

Perkins, D. (1986). *Design as Knowledge.* Hillsdale, New Jersey: Erlbaum Associates.

Simon, H. (1969). *The Sciences of the Artificial.* Cambridge, Massachusetts: MIT Press.

Slavin, R.E. (1986). *Using Student Team Learning.* Baltimore, Maryland: The Johns Hopkins Team Learning Project, Center for Research on Elementary and Middle Schools.

Wolf, D. P. (1992). "Opening Up Assessment." In *Performance Assessment,* Brandt, R., ed. Alexandria, Virginia: Association for Supervision and Curriculum Development.

3 A STRATEGY FOR
Excellent Teaching

chapter

t he best teachers bring learning to life with techniques and strategies that promote excellent student work and high teaching standards. For the innovative teachers who are the subject of this research, design-based curricula provide frameworks for achieving such excellence and high standards. While these teachers approach design on their own terms, they share a common concern for instruction that adapts to individual learning styles and an array of subjects.

The research for this book found considerable variation in how design is used in the classroom. Some teachers and students explore the modes of inquiry used by graphic designers, product designers, interior designers, and architects as strategies for learning new content and skills. They also may study the performances of everyday objects and places and the process for making decisions about visual communication, consumer products, and the built environment. Others use design as an active, hands-on approach to teaching and learning that motivates both teachers and students. In some cases, design is the subject of investigation; in other cases, it is the means of investigation.

It is clear from the classroom observations that design experiences invigorate teachers and students, transform the nature of teaching, and foster success for all types of learners. From the teacher's viewpoint, the use of design in K-12 classrooms achieves two important goals:

- Design-based teaching strategies support a broad range of student achievement by transforming the teacher from authority to facilitator, reaching all learner types, making learning active, and using technology in the service of ideas.

- Design-based teaching strategies build connections among teachers, subject areas, and the community.

Supporting A Range of Student Achievement

AS TEACHING objectives shift from instilling facts to improving students' thinking skills, educators find their roles in the classroom also change. Increasingly, teachers must prepare for instruction that guides rather than directs, that poses questions rather than provides answers. Through design-based pedagogy, teachers rediscover the art of teaching.

Transforming the Teacher's Role

The use of design has significant implications for the teacher, who moves from the role of omniscient authority to facilitator. In shedding the mantle of an expert who knows the answers to all problems, the teacher becomes a learner who shares with students an open mind about solutions to problems. While the overall achievement of learning outcomes are certain, there are no single "right" answers to design problems.

As Kim Turner, a 2nd grade teacher at Willamette Primary School in West Linn, Oregon, explains, "It's easier to be the expert, but the results are more powerful when I'm not. Rather than focusing on where I have to go next, I am able to hear children explaining their own thinking [about their design solutions] in ways that allow me glimpses into their development. These give me insight into my next moves to help them develop further."

Patricia Kadlec, a 4th and 5th grade teacher at Willamette, adds, "I am increasingly convinced I do my best teaching when I am on the edge of my own understanding."

Gail Aldridge, a 2nd and 3rd grade teacher at Willamette, reinforces the views of her colleagues. She remarks:

When I provide a framework for the children in my class and then step out of the way, I am amazed at what they can do! I can follow their progress in conversations and journals, and move in to assist in developing understanding or {to help with} a momentary frustration when the opportunity arises. In that way, I don't teach "beyond" them. There is a sense of relevancy. I am able to guide with questions, gestures, musings, and modeling, without the stultifying demands of direct telling. The {children} emerge on the other side of their questions with real answers of {their} own, with their self-esteem increased, and a belief they can tackle almost anything.

As facilitators, teachers urge students to evaluate the appropriateness of solutions they propose. In this role, teachers involve students in the process of "valuing" without imparting specific values themselves. They encourage and reward a variety of student approaches

Design experiences invigorate teachers and students, transform the nature of teaching, and foster success for all types of learners. Here, students at IS 246 in Brooklyn, New York, work together to build a chipboard model of the Bank of China in Hong Kong.

the teacher becomes a learner who shares with students an open mind about solutions to problems.

to problems rather than the single teacher-centered or textbook path. Teachers who use the design process as a map for classroom activity hold students accountable to student-authored performance criteria.

Barbara Van Wicklin, a gifted and talented teacher at Fillmore Central School in Allegany County, New York, affirms this view of design-based teachers as facilitators: "Design adds to my effectiveness because I become a facilitator rather than a knowledge giver. I allow for learning to take place rather than be the information giver…. I set judgment aside and join [students] in their quest. I am open to change and failure—and so are they."

A kindergarten teacher at Willamette Primary School recounts her transformation to a design-based facilitator: "My students were attempting to build tall buildings with newspapers when a little boy who did not know how to begin stopped his work in frustration. My first reaction was to tell him exactly how to roll the newspapers into tubes. However, I stopped for a moment and asked him what he was trying to do, and then we looked at columns and tall cans as possible models [for creating the form]. Although he still had difficulty with the mechanics of rolling, he knew what he wanted to do and asked a friend to assist him."

Teachers also report that design-based strategies energize their teaching. They find themselves creating new learning experiences that are appropriate for a particular group of children, rather than relying on tired exercises or lectures from a textbook. Even when repeating similar design assignments from year to year, teachers find that students ask different questions and invent new solutions. Mark Ceconi, a teacher at Daniel Webster Magnet School in New Rochelle, New York, says, "Using design also satisfies my personal creative needs, helping me to grow as an instructor by perpetuating my interest in the subjects I teach and confirming my ability to present them in ways I best know how."

Several teachers who use design activities in the classroom report that they avoid problems in student motivation that often occupy so much of teachers' attention. Van Wicklin talks about the joy of teaching motivated students: "I have found myself having to constrain enthusiasm rather than encourage it. My classroom always has

students working in it. They eat lunch there, spend free periods there, and many nights I have turned off the lights [and sent children home] because the janitors have to go home. Discipline problems are virtually nonexistent because of the high interest, hands-on experience the student is having."

Steve Brady, a technology education teacher at Eagle Ridge Junior High School in Savage, Minnesota, agrees: "During a design activity I find that the number of children 'on task' is greater than on nondesign activities." These teachers are among those who say that design-based teaching strategies allow them to focus on individual student achievement, rather than on group motivation and discipline.

Just as designers modify their practices based on the outcome of a design solution, teachers redesign learning experiences based on student performance. Because design problems can be multidimensional in the intelligences they tap and the skills they build, the teacher need not repeat assignments until students master content or skills. Instead, the teacher simply uses a new and interesting design task to develop the desired competency. Mark Ceconi offers an example from Daniel Webster Magnet School.

One child, in particular, comes to mind. She was a very quiet, introspective student with large gaps in language skills. She experienced a great deal of difficulty expressing her ideas in written or verbal form. Her drawings, however, were wonderfully embellished with rich detail and a sophisticated spatial awareness. In the writing process, she began using storyboard techniques to develop her ideas sequentially, first through drawing, and then by explaining each drawing using written detail. By the end of the year, she had developed a newfound self-confidence in her own abilities, and had grown immeasurably as a writer in her ability to express her ideas and views.

It is clear that Ceconi and other teachers who responded to the research survey maintain their interest in teaching largely because they see the profession as a creative challenge. Their roles as facilitators reduce redundancy in their daily practice and allow them to focus on the issues that attracted them to teaching in the first place.

Design helps me be more effective because not everyone learns the same way . . . I have been able to design many different ways of teaching an idea or method . . . If I didn't use "design" I would not reach many of the students in my class.

PATRICIA DICOSIMO,
9-12th grade art teacher,
Simsbury, CT

Reaching All Learner Types

Students exhibit varied capacities in different intelligences and individual preferences for learning in certain ways. Design-based experiences appear to reach a wider variety of learners than traditional methods of instruction, which favor the student who perceives information abstractly and processes it reflectively.

Howard Gardner argues that teachers should approach any topic worth teaching in at least five ways that reflect different intelligences. These include:

- **narrational,** presenting a story or narrative about the concept in question;

- **logical-quantitative,** invoking numerical considerations or deductive reasoning processes;

- **foundational,** approaching the concept from a philosophical and terminological perspective;

- **aesthetic,** emphasizing the sensory responses to surface features that capture the attention of students who favor an artistic stance to the experiences of living; and

- **experiential,** dealing directly with relevant materials that embody or convey the concept in a hands-on approach (Gardner 1991, pp. 244-246).

Gardner suggests that, taken together, these intelligences comprise the information and inquiry necessary to contribute to students' full under-standing of any topic. He maintains that "full understanding of any concept of any complexity cannot be restricted to a single mode of knowing or way of representation" (Gardner 1991, p. 247). He also believes studying a topic through multiple intelligences decreases the likelihood of misconceptions and stereotypes.

Mary Ann Chamberlain, a 5th grade teacher at Meadowthorpe Elementary School in Lexington, Kentucky, views design strategies as a way to engage students who excel in different intelligences: "Design allows me to build on each student's strengths as they are revealed through the process of design."

For example, when studying the way societies shape the built environment in response to cultural, social, and economic factors, Chamberlain incorporates the following activities to provide different points of entry to the subject and to encourage development of more than one type of intelligence:

- The examination of the past and present through book research on the structure and function of buildings. Students must present their findings visually, requiring deductive reasoning (diagrams showing how buildings stand up) and aesthetic understanding (records of visual and spatial properties such as massing, proportion, materials, scale, color, and ornament).

- The design and building of columns for use in buildings of a particular geographic region and time period. The column must sustain specified weight, but it also must be meaningful to people in the region. This activity provides both logical-quantitative and foundational points of entry to the study of built form. In building the model of the column, students deal directly with materials in an experiential mode.

- A five-day scavenger hunt for parents and students in which they must locate and identify specific architectural elements on a tour of homes in Lexington, Kentucky, built in the 1700s to the 1920s. This activity enters the discussion of the built environment through aesthetic experience.

Simsbury, Connecticut, high school teacher Patricia DiCosimo agrees that design helps her do her job well:

"Design helps me be a more effective teacher, because not everyone learns in the same way.... I have to be able to design many different ways of teaching an idea or method.... If I didn't use design, I would not reach many of the students in my class."

Several teachers note that the use of design in the classroom results in greater student success and increases the stature of students who do not excel in verbal or logical-mathematical skills. Julie Olsen, a 2nd and 3rd grade teacher at Hawthorne Elementary School in Madison, Wisconsin, makes this point: "Students who might otherwise get buried in a more traditional school... gain a lot of equity among their peers and confidence to learn in other areas.... The design problems we have studied are self-defined and require a lot of different approaches; there is no one 'right' answer. In many ways, all of the students are starting at the same point."

Tara Williams, a 7th grade social studies teacher in Warren County, North Carolina, notes that some of her students often have trouble demonstrating the depth of their understanding through words. She remarks that when her class uses newspaper to "model" various forms of government, "[I can] actually see what they [know]." Student models use torn and wadded paper to show the relative size and hierarchy among branches of government, centers of power, and the relationship of citizens to their government. The crudeness of the newspaper as a modeling material keeps student attention focused on the core issues, not on replicating irrelevant details or physical objects they associate with government. Unlike more traditional modeling or diorama projects, students need not have fine motor skills to succeed.

Teachers report that by providing multiple points of entry into subject matter, they deal effectively with student and teacher misconceptions, biases, and stereotypes. A study initiated by technology teacher Phil Nobile, English teacher Carol Ramsey, and physics teacher Tony Nicholson of Greenwich High School in Greenwich, Connecticut, looked for gender issues that might reinforce stereotypical notions that science and technology courses are not encouraged for young women. The Teachers of Problem Solving (TOPS) project was a collaboration between

teachers who use design

create greater

opportunity for special

students to have **successful**

learning experiences.

Greenwich Public Schools and Massachusetts Institute of Technology (MIT).

Nicholson sought greater participation in his design-based physics courses and arranged for teachers, students, and administrators to attend a day of study at MIT on strategies for encouraging female enrollment in technology classes. Returning to Greenwich, the teachers developed a course modeled on MIT's 2.70 Design/Build course, in which students work in teams to build a variety of products and structures. The faculty extended this approach by working with nearby elementary schools, having the high school students mentor the younger children on similar design projects. Nobile reports that TOPS boosted overall enrollment in technology at Greenwich High by 110 percent and female enrollment by 20 percent (Nobile 1994).

The Middle School Mathematics through Applications Project at the Institute for Research on Learning based in Menlo Park, California, also reports that their computer-oriented, design-based approach to the teaching of mathematics increases the participation of students who previously showed little interest in mathematics. They report that results are particularly striking among girls and students who speak English as a second language.

Because design activities accommodate students with different learning abilities, teachers who use design create greater opportunity for special students to have successful learning experiences. Along with teams of students from more than 30 schools in the greater Hartford area, students at the Special Education Learning Center participated in the Call to the Visionary Artist project, sponsored by the Architecture Resource Center of the Connecticut Architecture Foundation. The challenge was to design a building for a downtown riverfront site through coordinated disciplinary investigations. Art teacher June Bisantz-Evans and mathematics and science teacher George Macaruso work with students who have learning disabilities and behavioral problems, are at the 6th to 8th grade level, but whose performance is generally appropriate for the early primary years.

Bisantz-Evans and Macaruso report that subject matter that is usually a challenge for special students under traditional teaching strategies becomes easier when design is the focus of activity.

To meet social studies objectives, students explore the historical and social aspects of the project, such as the role of the river in the formation of the city, changes in city form as shown on maps, personal and family histories, shifting needs of the city across time, and physical changes in the buildings and city plan found through a walking tour with map and camera. In mathematics, class discussions lead to diagrams and measured models of columns and bridges. Students build small trusses that support weight based on their calculations. To meet art objectives, students brainstorm possible building designs and visualize their concepts through drawings and models, addressing practical concerns such as parking and safety, as well as aesthetic features of the building. To meet science objectives, students explore solar heating and the environmental need for plants in an indoor/outdoor park. Finally, in language arts, students write about why their building serves a purpose and in what way it successfully communicates its relationship with the river.

Bisantz-Evans and Macaruso also report, "The last phase of the project was the exhibition of all the citywide projects in a central location. When our students saw their model in the exhibit, they were truly proud. Self-esteem is an extremely important issue for these young people. Following this project to its conclusion and seeing with their own eyes that their work could hold its own with that of any other child was a real reward for all their effort. For us teachers, it was an equally powerful experience. We had not seen

the skills of some of these children prior to this project. One child who had poor reading and writing skills was recast after he and his friends realized that he had wonderful building skills."

Regardless of ability, students show preferences for ways to learn. Unfortunately, traditional lecture- and textbook-based classrooms favor one type of learner: the student who does well in reflective, abstract learning experiences. The use of design activities broadens the type of acceptable learning behavior in classrooms, allowing teachers to reach students in ways that correspond to their natural preferences.

Making Learning Active

Not all active learning is project based. Traditional laboratory experiments, technical drafting assignments, and some crafts lessons, for example, involve students in physical activity but are usually exercises in which the method is tightly defined and the outcome is known before students begin. While students' performance on exercises varies in quality, their solutions to the problem generally are the same.

In project-based learning experiences, on the other hand, the learner poses a problem for which there are many good answers. Projects usually stretch over a long period of time and require sustained concentration on various aspects

of the assignment. Students are active participants in devising a method for solving the problem and engage in distinctly different kinds of work across the span of the activity. Projects tend to require information and skills from a number of disciplines, encouraging students to move seamlessly across subject areas and to work in teams. Students frequently go through trial and error, testing solutions and making adjustments in their work based upon findings.

Design activities accommodate students with different learning abilities. These no-nonsense designers from the Hartford, Connecticut, Special Education Center pose with their carefully planned solution for a downtown development site.

47

Students at Bret Harte Elementary School in San Francisco designed and built this "magic suspension bridge." They wrote about the bridge, its qualities, and where in the world it could take them.

(Wolf 1992). Gardner calls this "situated learning," or learning that allows students to encounter the various forms of knowing operating together within the context of particular situations and to see how accomplished adult masters move back and forth spontaneously among ways of knowing and learning (Gardner 1990, p. 31).

Katherine Holtgraves, at Willamette Primary School, comments on situated learning: "I create opportunities for the children to engage in the real work of an artist, an engineer, architect or draftsman. Not only are they fascinated with these challenges, but it is through this kind of challenge that children relate learning to their own experience and realize the value of pursuing knowledge."

With very few exceptions, the research examples in this study are project-based and achieve learning outcomes that are consistent with the best project-based practices. The examples build on a long tradition of instruction in college-level design education and situate learning within the context of everyday problems. They demand integrated performance that draws from a variety of subjects and teaches students to observe, analyze, model, and test principles in action. The design process demands constant evaluation through prototype testing, group consensus-building, and personal reflection. It is

Rarely do two students arrive at the same solution to the problem.

Many educators consider project-based learning a particularly appropriate vehicle for education reform. David Perkins notes, "It is through doing that students best demonstrate that they can go reasonably beyond the information given, and that they can generalize, analyze, and invent" (1991, pp. 5-8). Dennie Palmer Wolf asserts, "Projects that have their foundations in the real world provide a model for young people of true enterprise that is likely to be encountered as they grow up. Through involvement in projects, students acquire skills in important areas such as research, evaluation, and production, and in the basic curriculum areas. They also obtain knowledge of what it means to carry out a significant undertaking with appropriate support and guidance"

clear from the study that teachers find design activities a natural process for introducing project-based learning into their classrooms.

Technology in the Service of Ideas

In all the schools visited, the research team observed the use of technology as an integral part of design activity. For many teachers, "technology" means computer hardware and software; for others it refers to tools as varied as hammers, cameras, and calculators. In the best circumstances, students learn to select and use technology in the service of ideas, in ways that transcend specific equipment and their application in particular assignments.

While many teachers report the use of close-ended computer software, such as SimCity, to teach design concepts, it is evident that computer technology in most design-based classrooms is simply a means to solving problems and not an end in itself. Many teachers cite the use of computers for modeling three-dimensional relationships, diagramming concepts, and animating dynamic principles. Open-ended programs that allow students to create their own text and illustrations help children of all ages explore and present their ideas.

Through arrangements with Autodesk, a manufacturer of graphics software used in K-12 settings as well as professional architecture and engineering firms, San Jose Middle School in Novato, California, and Dranesville Elementary School in Herndon, Virginia, expand students' repertoire of design media. Students at San Jose Middle School draw alternative arrangements of their classroom that better support their learning activities. At Dranesville, students use Autodesk software to write and illustrate reports and short stories. Students in both schools create storyboards and animations to demonstrate what and how they learn in various subjects. In Los Angeles at Open Charter Magnet School, students regularly develop stories and reports with elaborate diagrams and illustrations on Apple computers installed at their desks.

In Simsbury, Connecticut, art teacher Patricia DiCosimo teaches high school students graphic design through both traditional hand methods and professional design software programs. Students in Leslie Porges' 8th grade geography and civics classes in Chandler, Arizona, use the latest geographic information systems (GIS) software in their city planning and resource mapping activities. Across the country, numerous design and technology students also use Computer-Assisted Design (CAD) software to produce professional quality two- and three-dimensional representations of their design solutions.

Teachers also report that the use of technology in classroom design activities expands their own knowledge. In many cases, teachers become learners with their students, acquiring skills within the context of assignments. Teacher submissions for this study also indicate that teachers are frequently self-publishers who create learning materials that support design activities in their classrooms.

Teachers use both traditional hands-on methods and design software programs to teach their students. Students work with materials on a drawbridge design and construction (above) or use research and computer skills to create three-dimensional designs of the Golden Hinde (inset).

A Strategy for Making Connections

CURRENT REFORM initiatives signal fundamental changes in how teachers work. The creation and support of team approaches to instruction are hallmarks of reform efforts, diminishing the isolation of teachers from one another and building the individual classroom teacher's sense of belonging to a community of professionals. While team teaching is one approach, a coordinated group of individual classroom teachers who share common sets of students is more likely.

The development of design projects led by instructional teams within schools provides teachers with opportunities to coordinate their work across disciplines. One of the most common strategies is to use themes that unify several teachers' work with students through broadly-defined topical frameworks. Teachers select readings, illustrative examples, and assignments on the basis of the theme, encouraging students to make connections across traditional disciplinary boundaries. These teachers may still teach alone in their classrooms, maintaining students' focus on the way their discipline contributes to broader understanding of the issues at hand, but coordinate content and instructional planning with other teachers.

In some schools the goal is to integrate subjects; teachers ask students to draw from several subject areas in their investigation of problems that are not seated in a single discipline and that require integrated problem solving skills. In certain cases, teachers ask students to pose the problems or themes themselves.

Figure 3.1, adapted by Wake County, North Carolina, curriculum specialist Linda Isely from the work of Heidi Hayes Jacobs, shows current curricular profiles arranged according to the degree to which teachers of different disciplines collaborate.

While some teachers set the agenda for what students will learn, others ask students to play key roles in determining the timing, content, and approach to instruction. Despite the freedom in these classrooms, students are held accountable for achieving high standards of excellence and powerful learning. In other cases, students exercise their power to choose only within narrowly-defined options for subject matter and approach. The principles behind these approaches are to engage students in self-directed choices that connect content to their own lives and

Figure 3.1

Continuum of Options for Curriculum Design

Discipline Based

Focus is on strict interpretation of disciplines with knowledge presented in separate fields. Separate blocks of time during the school day.

Parallel Disciplines

Teachers sequence their lessons to correspond to lessons in the same area in other disciplines. Content does not change, only the order of teaching changes. The theory is that, with simultaneous teaching, students will make linkages.

Multi-disciplinary

Related disciplines are brought together in a formal unit or course to investigate a theme, issue topic, or problem. Linkages are made for the student by fusing the curriculum.

Interdisciplinary Units/Courses

Units or courses bring together the full range of disciplines in the school's curriculum for a period of time. Content and modes of inquiry are linked across the disciplines.

Integrated (Integrative)

The curriculum is focused on themes and problems that emerge from the child's world. The child poses questions around which the curriculum is built. In the extreme, the curriculum has no state or local bounds.

Design as a different approach to geometry. Mathematics can be understood visually, as well as computationally.

allow instructional strategies to arise naturally out of the complexity of meaningful problems.

Interdisciplinary and Cross-Disciplinary Teaching

While some teaching approaches make design a topic for investigation, others employ designerly modes of inquiry to explore traditional core subjects. The first approach may make design a discrete unit of study, but the latter strategy adds no additional discipline areas to the curriculum and helps teachers better achieve interdisciplinary and cross-disciplinary learning objectives within their respective teaching assignments.

Heidi Hayes Jacobs articulates the importance of creating curricula to offer a range of experiences that reflect both discipline-field and interdisciplinary orientations. Jacobs says, "By 3rd grade, children view subjects as changes in behavior, teacher attitude, areas of the room, and times of the day. Rarely does anyone explain to them the nature and power of the disciplines or how the subjects relate to one another…. This dual emphasis [singular focus on one disci-

At Dyker Heights Middle School, students demonstrate mastery of relevant disciplinary concepts through their participation in the school's Architecture and Design Program. These students display their model skyscrapers.

pline and interdisciplinary curricula] is different from past attempts at curriculum integration that viewed the two approaches as opposing points of view—through this century, there has been an unfortunate tendency for schools to go to extremes of either rigid subject isolation or strained, whimsical thematic instruction" (Jacobs 1991, p. 22).

Jacobs also attributes the high priority schools place on interdisciplinary curricula to an expansion of information: "While the school day has stayed about the same, knowledge has grown. The traditional confines of the school

day are literally bulging, and much of the newest, most valuable knowledge falls between the cracks of conventional subject areas." She also describes misconceptions about how well schools are doing at discipline-based teaching, saying, "If you go to your local high school science teacher and ask him to describe —not necessarily in great detail—the science that starts in the middle school, let alone the elementary school, he won't know" (Brandt 1991, p. 24).

David Ackerman and David Perkins wrestle with how to think about curriculum. They conceptualize curriculum on

two levels, curriculum and metacurriculum: "The curriculum is composed of substantive concepts and content of discipline-based fields. The metacurriculum is the thematic-based set of skills and strategies selected to help children acquire the curriculum content, and to develop the capacity to think and learn independently" (Ackerman and Perkins 1989, pp. 80-81). Perkins (1989, pp. 70-71) notes that a worthy integrative theme has "broad and pervasive application…reveals similarities and contrasts… and fascinates."

Perhaps the most striking characteristic of the use of design activities in schools is the ability to integrate knowledge across the boundaries of traditional school subjects. Design is inherently interdisciplinary. It draws upon content and skills in a variety of disciplines in the process of solving problems that usually reside within multifaceted contexts. These contexts involve physical, social, cultural, and temporal factors. While design problem statements define just how broad or narrow a context students will address, the criteria for evaluation usually reflect that design problems are situated within complex systems and require a variety of skills in their solution.

This study identified many cases in which teachers use design activities to build integration skills and content connections among disciplines. In numerous instances, teachers achieve mandatory curriculum objectives for their disciplines while unifying study across diverse subject areas.

Among the many examples of interdisciplinary and cross-disciplinary learning discovered through this research, the following example from Seattle teacher Deirdre McCrary is typical. McCrary uses the 5th grade social studies curriculum *Man: A Course of Study (MACOS)* to guide her year's work with 5th grade students. Integrating concepts from cultural and physical anthropology with biology, geography, math, and physics, McCrary emphasizes the designed world of habitats, tools, and shelter. Her assignment encourages students to build analogies among subjects that appear to be unrelated on the surface.

First, students look closely at five mammals of increasing {biological} complexity: the Pacific Coast salmon, herring gull, baboon, and chimpanzee, and finally they study a human population very different from their own— the Netsilik Eskimo. In following the concept of structure and function, {students} look at the design of these various animals and the work each must do. They compare the structure and function of Inuit clothing in their special environment, to the structure and function of a bird's feathers, to the needs served by the students' own clothing. Students also study the relationship between the need for shelter and the use of available materials. They might build birds' nests using sticks, leaves, moss, and mud, or construct model igloos from sugar cubes or marshmallows. In another design exercise, they take five materials—fish, caribou antler, tent thong, moss, and caribou bone—and design a sled that can carry all their belongings and yet be fully recyclable in the spring thaw.

While this example has an instructional richness derived from its use of information from many disciplines, many teachers also report using design activities to explore just a few subject areas. For example, at Gaithersburg Intermediate School in Gaithersburg, Maryland, art teacher Patrick O'Malley's class explores the form-structure relationships in the biological world through drawings and models. When building models and drawing maps of communities, Tim Valdez and Julie Olsen at Hawthorne Elementary School in Madison, Wisconsin, teach 2nd and 3rd grade students the mathematical concepts of scale, measurement, and geometry.

design problems are situated within **complex systems** and require a variety of **skills** in their solution.

53

The research team also found instances in which teachers from different disciplines share instructional responsibility for a single thematic unit. At Dyker Heights Middle School, 6th, 7th, and 8th grade teachers in mathematics, English, science, social studies, and technology collaborate on thematic instruction under the school's Architecture and Design Program, coordinated by 6th grade science teacher Manette Gampel. Design related to bridge construction, architecture, habitat, and public space are vehicles through which students demonstrate mastery of relevant disciplinary concepts.

In a multi-grade project to design a "Subterranean City," for example, students work in teams on sections of the city. The science component of the project explores why buildings stand up, strength of materials, principles of engineering, and the biological needs of inhabitants. In math, the students calculate live and dead loads, measure and construct I-columns from paper, and make scale drawings. In social studies, students research past architectural styles and modern transportation systems. The teachers jointly evaluate students on the basis of models, diagrams, and a research report describing the purpose

of each structure, the mathematical and scientific principles used, background information, and a bibliography. The project spans the year with different subject and grade level teachers devoting varying amounts of time to it each week.

Because of the scheduling complexities required to coordinate thematic instruction among teachers, this approach is most often used in self-contained classrooms where one teacher instructs a single group of students in all subjects, as in most elementary schools. Thematic units of study or projects are more common at the elementary levels. The strategy of using thematic units of study or projects becomes more challenging at higher grades, where emphasis on discipline-based instruction is also stronger. Yet, the continuing success of teachers and students in Dyker Heights' Architecture and Design Program shows that it can be done.

The next chapter provides specific examples of discipline-based curricular experiences in response to national standards. While the text describes many of these classroom projects under the headings of traditional disciplines, it is easy to find instances where other disciplines contribute to the success of the students' learning experiences. In some instances, teachers expand their disciplinary scope by enlisting teaching support from experts in the commu-

Design activities **encourage** **students** to draw from **richer** **sources** of information...

nity, building connections to content that may not be accessible through the school's own resources.

Connecting with the Community

One way to encourage children to be lifelong learners is to frame their learning experiences within the context of their own lives. As might be expected, traditional classrooms emphasize the acquisition of library reference information and often ignore important learning from other sources. Teachers who use design-based strategies, on the other hand, tend to have a more generous notion of "information." Visiting a landfill may better inform students' decisions about packaging design than watching a film about manufacturing. Interviewing a wheelchair user may elucidate issues of sociology, transportation, and community design more than any civics text. Design activities encourage students to draw from richer sources of information and value more than conventional sources of data.

The research team noted a variety of strong community connections among those schools and classrooms immersed in design activities. Design-based teachers frequently arrange interactions among their students and people from the community who provide materials, offer critiques, and serve as role models

and instructors. Teachers in the study encourage use of a broad range of information sources, relying on students' own experiences, interviews, and artifacts as frequently as textbooks for reference during design-based projects.

Many of the innovative teachers in this study take advantage of the professional resources in their communities, encouraging visits to the classroom. In Philadelphia, the Architecture in Education Program of the Foundation for Architecture uses graduate students and professional designers in architecture, landscape architecture, and planning to help teachers develop and carry out design-based units of study. The program also invites design professionals, city officials, and parents to view and critique student projects.

Gary Dewey, a 7th grade science teacher at Holland Christian Middle School in Holland, Michigan, brings designers from local firms, such as Herman Miller Furniture and Gentex, to his class to share their strategies for solving design problems and working in teams.

Two out of the 10 schools visited during the research study are adoptees of the national engineering firm CH2M Hill. Willamette Primary School has CH2M Hill engineers on its advisory board to provide ongoing consultation with staff on a range of issues and to

Gentex

CH2M Hill

. . . the presence of the engineer provides a link between the work students do and life outside of school and encourages young people to practice roles they may assume as adults.

DAVID PINKERTON,
Aurora, Colorado

KOPE

interact directly with students. At Dranesville Elementary, CH2M Hill engineers also make frequent visits to the classrooms to work with children.

David Pinkerton in Aurora, Colorado, invites a retired engineer to judge his students' Rube Goldberg machines. The engineer reviews the models, listens to students' explanation of the physics principles employed in their designs, and queries students about the possible applications of their work to problems of everyday life. Pinkerton reports that the presence of the engineer provides a link between the work students do and life outside of school and encourages young people to practice roles they may assume as adults.

Other teachers report that their classes visit places where design professionals work and observe their problem solving in action. These visits reinforce for students the notion that their pursuits are consistent with those of adults. As one 8th grade student noted, "I was shocked but really happy to see that Mr. Holt got as frustrated as I get when he was trying to figure out where to put

a stairway in his office building. He told me that these kinds of challenges never go away because each building is different."

In Peter Barricelli's 5th and 6th grade classes at several schools in Messalonskee School District in Oakland, Maine, students contact professionals inside and outside the classroom. Students interact with local professionals on an assignment that moves from the construction of a cube, to a room, to a building, to a whole city. With a surveyor, the children survey the school playground using professional equipment. An engineer shows them how to draw one of their house designs on the computer. Local architects and engineers critique their initial city plans, and the city planner provides useful information on town codes governing roads, sidewalks, and parking. A real estate lawyer from the community shows students how to register deeds and titles. Children responsible for building the town's hospital, fire station, and other buildings visit those facilities, analyze spaces and functions, interview users, and then return to school to develop their own designs. Students transfer deeds for the buildings and lots to the next year's class, which assumes responsibility for further modification of the model.

One of the strongest examples of teachers engaging students in their

community is the story of Hidden Hollow in Salt Lake City, Utah. Today, thanks to the inventiveness of teacher Sherri Sohm and the persistent awareness-raising efforts of KOPE (Kids Protecting Our Environment), the city consults 4th, 5th, and 6th grade students on decisions about the publicly owned land on the south side of Parley's Creek.

KOPE had its origins in the problem-solving lessons of Sohm's classroom at Hawthorne Elementary School. Twice a week Sohm works with accelerated students in the 4th through 6th grades, developing their critical thinking skills by challenging them to investigate environmental problems in their community. In 1990, when the school children discovered the paltry remnant of Parley's Creek struggling beneath construction debris, they proposed to rescue it.

Sohm structured research activities so that her students learned the history of the community and the creek, one of the terminal segments of the old Mormon Trail. Moreover, the site, now almost entirely ringed with buildings, had been one of the first settlements in the valley —Sugar, Utah—until Salt Lake City absorbed it early in the 20th century.

At the county records office, the students discovered that the strip of land surrounding the creek was a city park until 1957 and that there were now proposals to build a shopping mall,

KOPE students from Salt Lake City, Utah, display their 8-foot plan of Hidden Hollow and the surrounding business district.

which would bury the creek in a culvert and pave over the middle of the block for a parking lot.

Envisioning the miniature rift valley as a verdant respite from the surrounding business district, as a potential outdoor classroom for environmental studies, and simply as a great place to have fun, the students renamed it "Hidden Hollow." Sohm encouraged them to marshal information and allies from the community. First, the children organized KOPE and invited other ele-

mentary schools to lend their support and creative ideas. Then they assembled information about the site's resources and invited numerous experts including geologists, soil scientists, botanists, wildlife specialists, and the city's urban forester to the site to explore its hidden assets. With the help of landscape architects, the students also sketched and discussed design options for restoring the natural environment while making it accessible with trails, benches, and footbridges.

In the spring, developers met with the KOPE kids in the Hawthorne Elementary School Library and dismissed their dreams as too little too late. Undaunted, the students rallied public support for down-zoning the city-owned portion of land so that it could not be used for commercial development. Armed with research on city policies and a landscape architect's drawing of their design ideas, the students appeared before the City Council. Before an audience of several hundred

Landscape artist Jan
Striefel created this site
plan for Hidden Hollow,
using student ideas. The
plan helped the children
obtain grants for work on
the park.

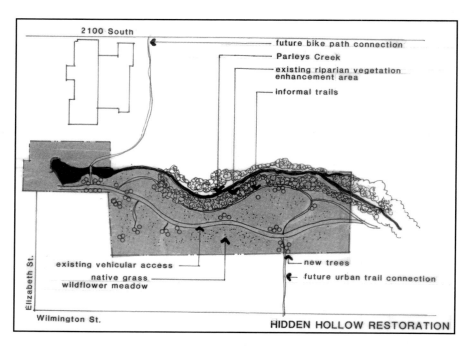

HIDDEN HOLLOW RESTORATION

2100 South

future bike path connection
Parleys Creek
existing riparian vegetation enhancement area
informal trails

existing vehicular access
native grass wildflower meadow
new trees
future urban trail connection

Elizabeth St.
Wilmington St.

adults and elementary school children, the Council approved KOPE's petition for the down-zoning.

Over the years, Sohm's classes have continued to use Hidden Hollow as a focus of their community-oriented problem solving. One group of students hosted a design workshop in Hidden Hollow, drawing together a variety of design professionals, parents, neighborhood residents, and local business people. Using maps of the city and their model of the 12-acre block, the children described their vision of the Hollow and invited public comment.

Under Sohm's guidance, the students developed an action plan for phased improvement of the Hollow, presented it to the city's departments of planning and public services, and won approval for their concept. Then the children learned how to write proposals for grants and in-kind donations. Their first proposal secured Community Development Block Grant funds to pay for the removal of 17,000 tons of construction debris and the installation of a gate to prevent further illegal dumping. Gradually, with the help of volunteers and their own "sweat equity," the students brought about the transformation they envisioned. The Utah National Guard and many others graded the terrain, planted trees, and laid out hiking/biking paths. Upcoming phases include the installation of security lights, an irrigation system, plants, benches, and interpretive kiosks.

With Hidden Hollow officially designated as open space and included in the city's Master Plan, the students turned their attention to the appearance of existing buildings, the proposals of various developers, and the opinions of business and home owners in the surrounding blocks.

Working with the Sugar House Chamber of Commerce, the students surveyed 269 businesses in the area and achieved an 80 percent response rate. The survey revealed strong support for completing Hidden Hollow and widespread recognition of the value added to the business district by this amenity. Students made models to illustrate how attention to building size, scale, materials, and placement of windows and doors helps new construction fit into the block and increases tenants' and customers' physical and visual access to the open space. These more recent explorations of development and design options are part of a larger study called "Sugar House Dilemmas," through which students at Hawthorne Elementary and their peers at Beacon Heights Elementary examine larger economic and social issues in the neighborhood, including crime and housing.

From a tiny stream to the complexities of urban development, the KOPE kids broadened their understanding of the interplay between natural and built environments and enlarged the context for their learning and community service. In the process, they educated and energized fellow students, teachers, parents, and a host of public and private sectors in Salt Lake City. The ripple effect of their work led to the *KOPE Kronical,* a bimonthly newspaper written by kids for kids. The paper chronicles not only the progress with Hidden Hollow but also the wide array of projects of environmental clubs established at other elementary and junior high schools in the area. Today the *Kronical* is distributed to 24,000 students in grades K-8 each school year. KOPE also initiated an annual series of Student Conferences on Sustainability at which children present projects that protect the area's natural and cultural resources.

Clearly, the use of design within and among disciplines presents new challenges for teachers and fundamentally alters their role in the classroom. Design also causes teachers to rethink the nature of assessment and the community context in which they teach. In accepting these challenges, however, teachers find renewed interest in teaching, view themselves as part of a community of creative professionals, and experience success in helping children reach their maximum potential.

References

Ackerman, D. and Perkins, D.N. (1989). "Integrating Thinking and Learning Skills Across the Curriculum." In *Interdisciplinary Curriculum: Design and Implementation,* Jacobs, H.H., ed. Alexandria, Virginia: Association for Supervision and Curriculum Development.

Brandt, R. (October 1991). "On Interdisciplinary Curriculum: A Conversation with Heidi Hayes Jacobs." *Educational Leadership* 49, 2: 24-27.

Gardner, H. (1990). *Art Education and Human Development.* Los Angeles, California: Getty Center for Education in the Arts.

Gardner, H. (1991). *The Unschooled Mind: How Children Think and How Schools Should Teach.* New York: Basic Books.

Jacobs, H.H. (September 1991). "The Integrated Curriculum." *Instructor* 101, 2: 22.

Nobile, P. (Summer 1994). Description of TOPS Project provided to NEA.

Perkins, D.N. (1989). "Selecting Fertile Themes for Integrated Learning." In *Interdisciplinary Curriculum: Design and Implementation,* Jacobs, H.H., ed. Alexandria, Virginia: Association for Supervision and Curriculum Development.

Perkins, D. (October 1991). "Educating for Insight." *Educational Leadership.* 49, 2: 5-8.

Wolf, D.P. (1992). "Opening Up Assessment." In *Performance Assessment,* Brandt, R., ed. Alexandria, Virginia: Association for Supervision and Curriculum Development.

4 DESIGN IN THE *Curriculum*

While a design approach to teaching is congruent with the objectives of interdisciplinary curricula, it also facilitates learning and the achievement of high standards within disciplines. The following sections describe learning expectations *within* disciplines and examples that support the notion that design experiences improve student performance in various subjects.

History and Social Studies Education

OPPORTUNITIES TO study design topics and use activities in social studies, geography, and civics abound, as suggested by the content and teaching scenarios in the voluntary national standards for these subjects. Topics may be drawn from the myriad of ways people use design to shape their environment and communicate their values: the design of graphic communications (print or electronic), product and packaging design, architecture, interior design, landscape architecture, historic preservation, town and city planning, natural resource conservation, and new development. The social studies standards are replete with examples of students analyzing the ways in which people, past or present, encode meaning in their communications, make products, design buildings, build bridges, and transform the landscape with cities and towns.

Engaging students actively in the design process, on the other hand, prompts them to consider how they would address various human needs, whether of their own or another time. They consider how the economy, culture, and technology of the time shapes the design response. They can build models of cities, plan for the mass production of products, and design posters to carry political messages. Such activities challenge students to articulate their own vision of how to

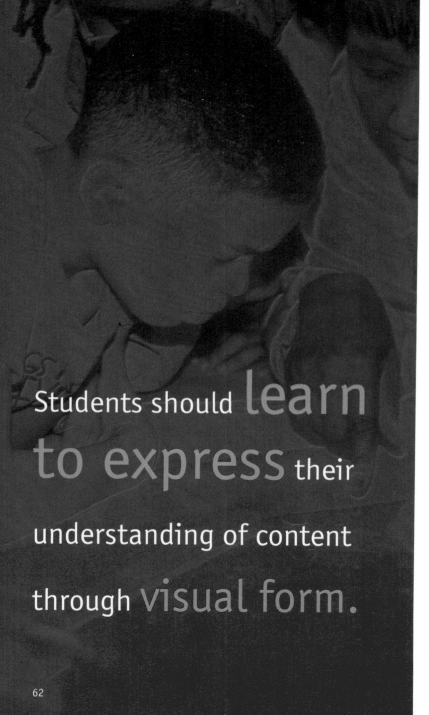

Students should **learn to express** their understanding of content through **visual form.**

preserve the best of what generations have left as a cultural legacy while creating a new, sustainable future. In response to the social studies standards' interest in analyzing group and individual needs, design activities can address how products and environments accommodate a variety of users who differ in their physical, economic, and social characteristics.

Throughout, the social studies and geography standards challenge teachers to develop student proficiency in the use of graphic communication techniques. Students should learn to express their understanding of content through visual form and to derive and analyze information from maps, charts, tables, and other graphic information. Both sets of standards encourage the use of technology, including CD-ROMs and the World Wide Web, in gathering and interpreting data. Regrettably, the standards stop short of asking teachers and students to study the principles of graphic design and to extend their abilities beyond mere mimicry of existing newspapers and Internet displays.

The geography standards are also replete with opportunities for teachers and students to explore the designed world and to exercise their own design talents. Among other things, "the geographically informed person knows and understands ... the spatial organization

of people, places and environments ... the processes, patterns, and functions of human settlements ... how human actions modify the physical environment" (Geography Education Standards Project 1994).

The geography standards further depict students progressing through increasingly demanding explorations of the built and natural worlds, paying particular attention to the ways in which their interdependence is discernible in spatial dimensions. Thus, from their earliest years, students use mental maps to organize information about people, places, and environments. They can make physical maps and scale models of their community, showing different land uses. By 4th grade, they should show ways in which humans adapt to environmental conditions through the design of clothing and shelter, understand the effect of natural resources and transportation technologies on the location of communities, and compare areas within their own community in terms of different facilities and infrastructure.

In subsequent years, the standards expect students to understand the demographic and economic determinants of business location, the relationship of transportation types to urban and suburban growth, and the impact of that growth on agriculture, watersheds, and specific ecosystems. In 5th through 8th grade, they should be able to identify cultural elements in the landscape, from local landmarks to architectural styles to patterns of farming and settlement; assess the environmental impact of using wetlands for recreation or building; and solicit and examine people's differing opinions about the use or misuse of resources.

By high school, students should be able to analyze the structure and shape of cities and predict the impact of changes in population, transportation, and economic activity. Ultimately, they should develop policies on resource management, design alternative systems, and carry their debate about sustainable development into the public arena.

National Standards for Civics and Government, from the Center for Civic Education, asserts that preparing students for a life of civic and political participation is a critical mission for education. While articulating the knowledge students should master and the intellectual skills they should develop, the Center also encourages teachers to use a variety of dynamic models to cultivate and strengthen the participatory skills essential to civic life. The standards call for students to conduct research in the community; take and defend positions; meet with different stakeholders; and try their

hands at coalition building, conflict resolution, and governance (Center for Civic Education 1994, p. 5).

The research for this book uncovered many examples of teachers using design activities to achieve history and social studies objectives. Epiphany School in Seattle, Washington, uses a graphic design problem to teach elementary school students about ideological positions in World War II and about the power of visual persuasion. Deirdre McCrary's students study *Life* and *Time* magazines from the 1930s and 1940s and then describe the connections advertisers made between their products and the war. They study the visual vocabulary of the period and make notes about images and type styles. Students then create propaganda posters for either an Axis or Allied power. The posters are intended to recruit soldiers or volunteers, persuade citizens to buy war bonds, urge greater industrial production, incite emotions over the war, inform people of substitutes for rationed food and fuel, or convince people to conserve resources. "Through this activity," McCrary states, "students also become more discriminating viewers of contemporary commercial and political advertising."

Barbara Clark, a social studies teacher at Sequoyah Middle School in Broken Arrow, Oklahoma, requires students to select an explorer for the focus of their study. After researching the explorer's life and travels, students have the option to design and write a travel brochure encouraging others to join his expedition; write and videotape a news broadcast about the explorer's discovery, as it might be heard in the period under study; or design a mural that records the explorer's adventures. These activities require students to reframe textbook research in terms of audience and the method of reporting. Unlike typical research reports, the design products

In making this model of a Greek Revival house, students at Hawthorne Elementary School in Madison, Wisconsin, learned why this style of architecture appealed to citizens of the early United States

demand active student attention to how others perceive information and the impact of the reporting format on content structure.

Teachers in this study report that reading a book about another culture does not have the same impact on students as does studying actual artifacts or creating objects of that culture. To produce design artifacts, students must understand the culture's world view, its essential beliefs and customs, its physical setting, and available materials and technologies. Appropriately structured, these are not simply exercises in which students physically replicate cultural objects, but activities that reveal deep social structures and beliefs. They illustrate how cultures encode artifacts with strongly held ideas and aspirations.

At Union Grove High School in Union Grove, Wisconsin, Terry and Karen Crown use design to integrate art and global studies. Students conduct traditional library research on geographic regions of the world, compare cultural characteristics through analysis of indigenous design, and create artifacts for each region they study. For example, students examine different hats from around the world; understanding comes through an analysis of materials, environment, the hat's shape and methods of construction, and pupose.

Other teachers report that concerns such as the design of shelter and cities are points of entry into studies of culture and settings other than their own. At Hawthorne Elementary School in Madison, Wisconsin, Julie Olson's 2nd and 3rd grade students study the neighborhoods in which they live, but focus on common needs that people throughout the world have for shelter. They find they can use design to understand and appreciate differences in culture by comparing needs people share in common.

Alison Clark's 6th grade class at Louis Armstrong Middle School in East Elmhurst, New York, draws plans and builds models of Sumerian, Egyptian, Greek, and Roman cities; discusses the influences of environment and available materials on the design of the city; and writes city planning regulations. They then compare these ancient cities to their own neighborhoods.

Donna Banning, an art teacher at El Modena High School in Orange, California, uses a social studies context to structure her art history lessons.

While much of art history instruction in high school classrooms focuses on the visual characteristics of an art movement, as exemplified by the work of a few individuals, Banning places designed objects and environments in broader social, cultural, and historical contexts. In describing a typical project, she says, "Art history students study the changing attitudes toward worship over time by researching the variety of spaces used for that purpose. From early Paleolithic cultures to contemporary communities, there have been many different places of worship designed and constructed to meet the particular needs, available space, philosophy, economy, and materials of a given people." Banning uses designed objects and environments to invert the traditional hierarchy of high school art history, making the social, cultural, and historical context the center of discussion and the objects or environments simply evidence of change. She moves across time in exploration of the changing attitudes toward a social-cultural issue, rather than through a tightly defined, artist-centered chronology of objects that may have few social or cultural concerns in common.

Social, cultural, and technological history come together for students participating in the annual "Create a Landmark Contest" sponsored by the Historic Landmarks Foundation of Indiana.

Contemporary environments also serve as rich resources of information about the students' own culture, as well as opportunities to practice research and decision making skills. The social studies curriculum at Public School 145M in New York City requires that teacher Felice Piggott cover the topics of neighborhood and community with her 2nd grade students. Piggott interprets this curriculum requirement through a mapping activity in which her students first analyze the content of their community (residences, services, landmarks) on individual tally sheets compiled during a walk through the neighborhood. On maps drawn after studying how

architects depict space from aerial viewpoints, the students record symbols that stand for their tallies. Finally, they go back out into the neighborhood to check the accuracy of their maps and compare different analyses by students in their class. This translation of a walking experience into a two-dimensional representation of the journey focuses student attention during and after the tour. They learn important skills in encoding and decoding symbolic form and the two-dimensional depiction of three-dimensional space. This influences how they later interpret graphic representations of ideas and relationships among ideas, an important skill that is

critical to understanding data in the social sciences.

In Plano, Texas, Ann Tucker teaches Texas history at Haggard Middle School where a core objective in her 7th grade class is to identify the structure and functions of local, county, and state governments, including city planning. Tucker encourages her students to interview city employees to gain a variety of perspectives as they work in research groups.

Following a presentation of team findings, the teacher asks each student to plan and design an ideal city using information presented by the teams. In addition to drawing a detailed plan of

Students at Haggard Middle School in Plano, Texas, study local and state government, including city planning. As they work on their own city plans, students often consult with local officials to gain a variety of perspectives.

the proposed city, the student writes a narrative describing the type of government, services, financing, and growth strategies for the community. The class evaluates designs on the basis of content, location and inclusion of services, feasibility of government and taxing functions, and innovations in transportation and communication.

The strategy of involving students in the planning and design of a city also works for Eugenia Jameson, a sociology teacher at Plano Senior High. Her curriculum requires that students

understand the influence of history and geography on cultural values and norms, the dynamic interaction between economic development and social stratification, the evolution of social and governmental institutions to meet basic needs, the urbanization process, and the influence of changing technology on all of these elements. Jameson also expects students to develop skills in problem solving and citizenship through participation in activities such as role-playing, debates, and group projects.

In teams, students design and make a model of their own city. In an accompanying narrative they must name the city, define its present population and a 20-year projection, and explain how the city's design will accommodate growth, respond to natural features, and relate transportation, infrastructure, housing, jobs, and recreation. Students consider the needs of different age, ability, and income groups. In their final report they describe the governmental structures required to make their city work. At the end of the year, members of Plano's planning commission and city staff critique both middle school and high school projects and present awards for the best city plans.

In contrast to planning cities from scratch, Leslie Porges' 8th grade civics and geography classes at Bogle Junior High School in Chandler, Arizona, tackled the complexities of planning for South Chandler, a 16-square mile area quickly turning from a rural to urban community. Armed with maps from local government, Porges' students first inventoried South Chandler by bus, then created a more detailed classroom map showing topographic features, roads, and existing development.

Based on population projections, the students knew they had to plan for an average density of 3,500 people per square mile. They created zones for clean, high-tech industry along the major freeway and railroad tracks, placed higher density multi-income housing near these employment centers, and allowed for lower density housing further out.

Throughout their project, the students consulted a variety of people in the community to make their decisions about commercial development, professional offices, schools, recreational spaces, and medical facilities. They also determined where to locate utilities, fire stations, and bus stops.

The students learned that careful analysis of traffic patterns, land values, and community demographics forms the basis for most development decisions.

To encourage nonpolluting forms of transportation, they proposed adding walking and biking paths in the right-of-way along most major corridors. To conserve water, mitigate against heat build-up, and make the city attractive, they also called for landscaping with drought-resistant plants on commercial street frontage, with more extensive buffers around industrial sites and other large facilities.

Though working with rudimentary tools, Porges' classes produced a detailed and sophisticated plan, which won awards from the American Planning Association and the American Express Corporation. Prize money from the latter's national geography competition enabled Porges to acquire a computer and mapping software. Succeeding classes now continue city planning activities with the ability to produce professional-looking documents that identify a wide range of urban design elements.

At the Ethical Culture School in New York City, 5th grade teacher Hettie Jordan-Vilanova uses a design project to focus student attention on the future and how the decisions made by our own culture will communicate the content of our lives to future generations. She asks students to design and build an archaeological dig site for the year 3000. "What artifacts have survived?

What do they say about the culture? What do they tell you about how these people lived?" Jordan-Villeco's assignment results in scale models of the site and short stories written from the perspective of the archaeologist who makes the discovery. This activity points out to students that we learn history not only through major events and people described in books but also by studying the everyday aspects of people's lives, including our own.

Because design objects and environments both reflect and shape the culture in which they are produced, they prompt lively discussions and comparisons. Students gain insight into worlds other than their own and learn to appreciate differences as well as identify common concerns among people.

In one project, 5th graders at the Ethical Culture School in New York City analyzed their neighborhood needs and then designed and created models for an interactive science and technology museum (above) and for a community center and hospice (left).

67

"...for the natural world everywhere displays the significance of the concepts of mathematics, and the designed world is largely dependent upon them."

OECD, *Changing the Subject,* 1996, p. 89

THE ENGLISH LANGUAGE Arts standards, published by the National Council of Teachers of English and the International Reading Association in 1996, provide clues to the importance of visual thinking to reading and writing.

The standards show interest in students posing problems and speculating on their solution by gathering, evaluating, and synthesizing information from print and nonprint text, artifacts, and people. The standards pay special attention to the "complexity and creative potential of human problem solving" (International Reading Association and the National Council of Teachers of English 1996, p. 38), as well as the presentation of clear and convincing arguments necessary to achieve results. The preceding examples of design activities in which students become participants in their own communities involve situations in which students use interviews and persuasive language in support of their ideas for change.

Spanning grade levels, the standards document refers to mastering visual as well as verbal language. Presenting stories and information in nonprint media, including film and video, receive considerable attention in discussions of language structure and interpretation. These references, and the design examples throughout this book, support the notion that successful students exercise more than verbal and computational vehicles of thought, and that doing so actually enhances all understanding. In addition, the standards call for students to extract information from maps, charts, photographs, and other graphic material and to use these forms of visual representation in developing persuasive arguments and effective communication.

Michael Joyce, Vassar professor of English and author of *Of Two Minds: Hypertext Pedagogy and Poetics,* goes a step further in discussing the visual aspects of reading and writing. Joyce describes a technologically induced shift in human consciousness that theorists believe is as profound as the historic move from oral to print communication. In a hypertext computer environment, readers choose the order in which they read and participate in the construction of meaning. Writing becomes visual, as well as verbal, demanding attention to both the form and content of text. What Joyce describes are tasks previously assigned to graphic designers, visual communication professionals who control reader's eye movements, amplification of certain ideas, and juxtapositions of pictures and words that create new or modified meanings. Joyce and others believe new technology fundamentally redefines reading and writing to include a visual

...successful students exercise more than verbal and computational vehicles of thought...

command of language. In this context, the fit between design activities and language arts may be tighter than it first appears (Joyce 1994).

The research for this book revealed many examples in which teachers use technology in the development of writing skills. Although the most common examples include the authoring of illustrated texts or multimedia scripts that students later animate on the computer, others use design experiences to broaden students' sensitivity and understanding of subject matter.

At Willamette Primary School in West Linn, Oregon, 2nd and 3rd grade teacher Katherine Holtgraves asks students to write the story of "mechanimals" at the same time they are building a cam-driven, wooden toy. Their efforts result in first person narratives told from the perspective of the animals. This example illustrates both Joyce's comments on the need to address a nonlinear approach to content development (manifested in

the "question web" described below) and the use of design to acquaint students with the subject of their writing.

The children developed a question web about animals in general. They used the questions that intrigued them and added more specific ones to generate individual question webs about their chosen animal. Each child gathered information through a text search and kept notes in the learning logs. We listened to several passages selected for their narrative qualities and developed a list of those common features to understand "narrative" writing. We used the same process to experience "first person perspective." The children drafted their animal information in that style, decided on pagination and accompanying illustrations, and designed borders that were symbolic or foreshadowing (both ideas based on published books we perused).

We worked through inquiry to explain how the rotation of an off-set wheel moves a vertical shaft up and down. They listed the essential elements of that system and created a materials list. The children drew their

ideas of the mechanics and later incorporated that system into a design of their own, illustrating their animal in its habitat. Their journals housed all of their working drawings and notes.

Gail Aldridge, who also teaches 2nd and 3rd grade students at Willamette, reinforces the importance of the design process to the teaching of writing, "[The students] think through our design process and plan ahead using a sequencing strategy. We have carried that structure over to our writing. And our draft-revision processes in writing are natural connections to our process with three-dimensional construction. We have also developed a 'habit' of trying a variety of approaches or layouts before deciding on one, and keeping a working portfolio of options in case we need to dip into it for alternative ideas as we go."

Patricia Kadlec teaches older students at Willamette. She says, "I share with my children graphic structures for organizing information and setting up their writing. We use webs, flowcharts,

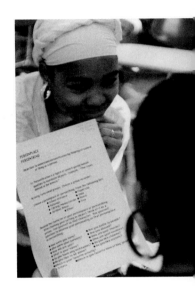

A left-handed writer solves the problem of smearing ink while writing. She designed a glove that moves above the page on wheels.

morphological analysis charts, and Venn diagrams. These are visual designs that we use in many ways. I make time in our busy schedules to honor crafts-manship, working though draft stages to final copy with plenty of time for reflection, response, and revision. Just as in adult design studios, the critique that children receive from peers can be used in the present project or tucked away for later reference. We strive for quality and our efforts pay off in pride, rising standards, and new discoveries."

At Daniel Webster Magnet School in New Rochelle, New York, Mark Ceconi's 4th grade students design and make comic books that illustrate their own narratives about superheroes. Using a writing technique called "semantic mapping," students brainstorm the traits of their characters in diagrams with radiating notes and sketches about visual details and behavior. They organize attributes in charts under sections titled costume design, superpowers, and alter-ego. Then they build a visual

storyboard of the narrative that reveals their characters' lives.

Design shares with writing an interest in metaphor. Developing analogies is a common problem-solving strategy for designers; they ask how the demands of a problem situation are like other things that provide similar performances. Research shows that the ability to make analogies is a strong characteristic of creative people and develops through practice. Rubie Blount, a 9th grade English teacher at Hillside High School in Durham, North Carolina, asks students to develop visual analogies as prompts for their writing assignments. She says, "Using direct analogy (a door is like a lid), personal analogy (if I were a door I'd be revolving), and compressed conflict (a door is an 'open barrier') as a prewriting activity is a fun way to get kids to think creatively . . . Comparing the school hallway to Main Street forced us to extend our thinking to the limits. Because we initially felt the two were not a lot alike, we had to change our way of thinking to be more inclusive."

Mathematics Education

CONCERN OVER mathematics education, expressed by the National Council of Teachers of Mathematics (NCTM) and the larger professional community, resulted in new national goals for mathematics curricula. These include: creating connections to other subjects and to the world outside the classroom; emphasizing complex, open-ended problem solving; and increasing communication and reasoning about mathematics (National Council of Teachers of Mathematics 1989). NCTM recognized that reconnecting mathematics to everyday living is paramount to engaging young people, especially female students and minorities.

Lisa Leonard, a 6th grade mathematics and reading teacher at Derby Middle School in Birmingham, Michigan, shows how her two subject areas inform students' design and construction of bridges from toothpicks. Students begin by reading stories about a man who builds bridges from match sticks and a book about the construction of the Brooklyn Bridge. Working with the technology teacher, Leonard shows student "companies" how to draw plans for their own bridge designs on their assigned sites. Given a budget, students must order materials, maintain balance sheets, and chart the progress of the job. Upon completion of their bridge, each student company predicts the weight its bridge will bear and where it will rank among the successful solutions in the class. Accountants, civil engineers, carpenters, and a local bridge builder join the class for discussions and a final test of each design's structural capacity.

The research team heard from many teachers that the new goals for mathematics education are consistent with the achievements of students who engage in design-based learning. Primary teachers most commonly report the use of design activities to teach measuring and calculation. A 1st grade teacher at Dranesville Elementary School in Herndon, Virginia, uses the construction of LEGO villages to teach children about scale and proportion. Each child must build a different element of the village, proportional in size to the other elements. Soon a classroom set of rules for relative size evolves.

Researchers observed sophisticated uses of design for teaching mathematics at Chipman Middle School in Alameda, California, and at Roosevelt Middle School in San Francisco, California. Both schools are participants in the Middle School Mathematics through Applications Project (MMAP), developed by the Institute for Research on Learning in Menlo Park, California. The 8th grade classes of Bob Bergin and Ramona Muniz use MMAP-designed software tools to support their practical inquiries. For example, MMAP's ArchiTech, a drawing and spreadsheet computer program, allows students to design floor plans of buildings; investigate the effects of changes in heating and insulation values; and calculate measurements, scale, and proportion.

In the early lessons, groups of students design a research station for eight researchers in Antarctica. They work with an architectural program that aids them in drawing the living quarters and a research facility. Students collectively design and draw a proposed solution on the computer. They then calculate the costs to build it, including the walls, windows, and furniture. Costs drive modifications in construction.

In later lessons, students calculate the costs of heating the facility. They then find the best R-value of insulation for reducing heating and building costs. Students defend this optimal insulation level through mathematical and real-world arguments.

MMAP research findings and testimony from teachers suggest that the program encourages enthusiastic participation of students who never before showed an interest in mathematics. Jim Greeno, a research fellow at the Institute for Research on Learning and the Margaret Jacks Professor of Education at Stanford University, offers

success stories about students who were previously "written off" by math teachers.

He says, "The MMAP approach reorganizes students' relationships to learning. My general impression is that the student who is alienated by the authoritarian structure of math and science, which have been taught in ways that *reek* of authority, may do better under the MMAP approach. In open-ended problems, one of the things that gets opened up is the social structure." Greeno goes on to say, "If problems are specified for students to solve and students are given the facts and the procedures to solve them, they don't have an opportunity to identify a significant problem from a trivial one. The studies we have on people in the work environment clearly indicate that recognition of important problems and figuring out what to do in response to them is critical to success."

Teachers also use design strategies to teach high school mathematics. Joanne Stanulonis, a mathematics teacher at Crossroads High School in Santa Monica, California, uses several design assignments in her classrooms. One project asks geometry students to explore the calculation of perimeter, area, volume, ratio, and proportion in the construction of a model house. The students determine the quantity of materials needed, make scale drawings,

calculate the appropriate BTUs for cooling the house, determine the amount of water needed to fill the pool, and tally estimates within budget requirements.

In another assignment on transformational geometry, Stanulonis's students create Escher-like tessellations, rotating, reflecting, and vertically and horizontally transforming functions depicted in the Cartesian plane. Stanulonis says, "[Students] see these activities as a 'break' from learning! Ha! Are they fooled! Some of the greatest learning and hardest lessons emerge from these design lessons! ... More importantly, students discover they can 'work it out' with a peer by merely discussing the problem, tossing it back and forth."

According to the Third International Mathematics and Science Study (TIMSS), funded by the National Science Foundation and released in October, 1996, U.S. schools introduce students to a greater number of mathematics concepts than their counterparts in other countries, but seldom do American students explore these concepts in depth. The study of 41 countries found that American students focus on mastering mathematics procedures rather than on making sense of their application in everyday situations. According to Ken Travers, professor of mathematics education at the

University of Illinois/Champaign and a member of the TIMSS steering committee, the articulation of content standards and benchmarks for mathematics in the United States is "right on track," but the transformation of actual classroom practice lags behind. "We talk about the importance of engaging students, of collaboration, and of problem-solving," Travers notes. "The videotapes [from this study] provide ample evidence that the Japanese teachers are already doing this" (*Education Update,* January 1997). What is needed, the TIMSS researchers conclude, is to make content more relevant to students by linking it to their personal lives, extending learning beyond the classroom, and encouraging more in-depth exploration.

Science Education

IN 1985, THE American Association for the Advancement of Science (AAAS) launched Project 2061, a multi-year initiative to encourage systemic educational reform. In *Science for All Americans,* project director James Rutherford and co-author Andrew Ahlgren subsequently set forth the rationale for this ambitious undertaking. In it they decried traditional teaching methods that emphasized "the learning of answers more than the exploration of questions, memory at the expense of critical thought, bits and pieces of information instead of understanding in context, recitation over argument [and] reading in lieu of doing" (AAAS 1989, p. viii). The authors called for a new goal: to develop scientifically literate citizens who understand our evolving technological society, exercise wise judgment in the public realm, and play productive roles in the economy.

To remedy this situation, Project 2061 promotes education reform with the goal of developing the scientifically literate person as "one who is aware that science, mathematics, and technology are interdependent human enterprises with strength and limitations; understands key concepts and principles of science; and uses scientific knowledge . . . for individual and social purposes" (AAAS 1989, p. vii). The way to achieve such literacy, according to Project 2061, is

Students at Hemingway Elementary School in Ketchum, Idaho, study acceleration and momentum by solving problems in the design of a roller coaster track.

to teach principles and processes, not in the abstract, but in a variety of everyday contexts with which students are familiar. AAAS encourages teachers to involve students in identifying problems, framing questions, actively investigating, generating and testing alternative solutions, and describing outcomes using a full range of visual and mathematical models.

Project 2061 has had widespread influence on science reform efforts in the United States. In articulating its vision of appropriate "scope, sequence, and coordination" of science education,

the National Science Teachers Association (1992) endorsed the approach to content espoused in *Science for All Americans.* Similarly, Project 2061's 1993 publication of *Benchmarks for Science Literacy* influenced the development of national voluntary content standards then underway.

Benchmarks states up front that the goal of science literacy is in part to help people "make sense of how the natural and designed worlds work" (AAAS 1993, p. xi). In presenting guidelines for what students should know and be able to do in science, mathematics, and

Sixth graders at Dyker Heights Intermediate School in Brooklyn, New York, designed this catapult for the 1996 Eureka Competition.

teaching must involve students in inquiry-oriented investigations in which ... they apply science content to new questions; they engage in problem solving, planning, decision making, and group discussions; and they experience assessments that are consistent with an active approach to learning" (National Research Council 1996, p. 20).

The authors of the *National Science Education Standards* acknowledge that children in kindergarten through 4th grade can understand and carry out design activities before they can engage in direct scientific inquiry. Thus design serves as the vehicle for gaining direct experience with materials and the forces of nature. From the earliest age, students can examine familiar products, such as zippers, can openers, bridges, and cars. They can identify the problem each design solves, describe the materials used, and analyze how well the design performs.

Very young children can also design their own communi-  cation, products, and environments. Through the design process, children learn how to analyze constraints, such as cost or safety; to communicate their ideas verbally and graphically; and to work independently and collaboratively with a spirit of

technology by the end of grades 2, 5, 8, and 12, this tool for curriculum development devotes an entire chapter to exploring aspects of the designed world.

The National Research Council of the National Academy of Sciences joined the voices of reform by calling for voluntary national standards for science education (National Research Council 1996). Echoing Project 2061's insistence that students be engaged, the standards say, "Hands-on activities are not enough—students must have 'minds-on' experiences. Science

mutual respect for alternate approaches to the same problem.

In grades 5-8, students differentiate between science and technology. They understand that scientists propose explanations for questions about the natural world, while designers and engineers propose solutions that respond to human problems, needs, or aspirations. They learn that design solutions must work within the constraints of nature, taking into consideration the properties of materials, varied physical abilities of different people, the force of gravity, and so forth.

Like their counterparts in earlier grades, these students also analyze designed products, environments, and systems in the world around them. They develop their own solutions to complex problems and extend their explorations beyond products to structures, landscapes, and assembly lines. They learn to interview potential users and to probe constraints, including those that arise from societal preferences (for efficiency, safety, etc.) and those embedded in the natural world (such as the effect of natural forces or the durability of materials).

In general, the National Research Council finds that many high school students harbor a popular but erroneous view that equates science with progress but technology with environmental

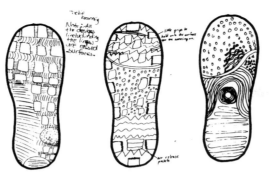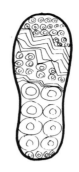

problems. At the same time, they "respond positively to the concrete, practical, outcome orientation of design problems before they are able to engage in the abstract, theoretical nature of many scientific inquiries" (National Research Council 1996, p. 191).

Design activities are powerful illustrations of the ways in which science and technology shape one another. By dissecting the processes and choices that led to design solutions and by analyzing their consequences, students understand that all technological solutions carry risks and benefits. Moreover, they learn that the solution to one problem may illuminate the need for further scientific research or new technology.

By being both judicious and creative, teachers can use even a limited number of design activities to reveal multiple

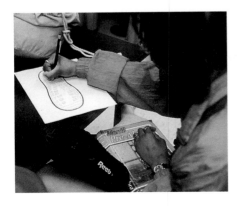

facets of science. The standards suggest, for example, that students might analyze features of different athletic shoes, measuring the friction caused by various tread designs and exploring constraints imposed by the needs of different sports movements, the human anatomy, and different materials.

The picture of high school science education painted by the *National Science Education Standards* is exciting and multidimensional. The standards encourage students to tackle more complex design problems than in earlier grades and to probe the myriad of influences that shape design criteria and constraints. The standards expect students to analyze the costs and benefits of design solutions and to document the evolution of their thinking and creativity, using drawings, three-dimensional models, and if possible, computer-assisted design. At the center of this learning, students come to understand the interconnections of science and technology, while also gaining a deeper appreciation of the value and

necessity of knowledge and skills in other disciplines.

Teachers contacted in the research for this book provide evidence that the goals of science education reform can be achieved in typical classrooms with students who might view science as a formidable hurdle under more traditional teaching approaches. At Sam Houston High School in Lake Charles, Louisiana, students in Linda Wygoda's chemistry and environmental science classes build structures from straws, make composite materials, and produce multimedia presentations on weather, molecular structure, and kinetics. Wygoda values the design approach, especially with students who are apprehensive about science. She says, "Design has been an outlet for my creativity as well as that of my students. I wouldn't teach any other way."

At Lakeview High School in Columbus, Nebraska, Ed Kinzer's 10th-12th grade students in a science research class carry out independent projects. Student Mark Moeller

Any activity that causes students to think and make is good. If the activity causes them to rethink and redo, it's even better....When students design, build, use and test their own projects, it's the best that science education gets.

PAUL BURTON, 7-8th grade teacher, Tucumcari, NM

HOW MANY
TIMES ITS
WEIGHT CAN
STYROFOAM
LIFT?

student
discovery
and invention

designed, built, and tested an infrared walking stick for visually-impaired individuals. The user presses a switch in the stick, sending out beams of light. Reflecting back from objects, the beams set off one of three buzzers depending on the distance of the object. Moeller's design won national awards for science research and invention.

Mark Ceconi, a 4th grade teacher at the humanities-centered Daniel Webster Magnet School in New Rochelle, New York, teaches the principles of aerodynamics through the design of model hang gliders built from straws, tissue paper, and pipe cleaners. Students learn about lift, drag, hot air currents called "thermals," and how the actions of the pilot change the movement of the aircraft. Throughout the lesson, students study analogous structures in birds: hollow bones, skeletal structures, and feathers.

Manette Gampel, a science teacher at Dyker Heights Intermediate School in Brooklyn, New York, uses a design project entitled Building Biomes to teach the mandated curriculum in the natural sciences. The intent of the project is to explore the interdependency of plants and animals in an ecosystem. Students select a land or water biome, conduct research in the library, and record the plant and animal life that will thrive in the biome's climate and geography. They also study human inhabitants' behavior, including occupations, food procurement, and housing. Students then design and construct their own biomes, choosing plants and animals they predict will produce a balanced ecosystem. They consult with pet stores, plant nurseries, and the Brooklyn Botanic Garden. Using computers, the students keep daily records of soil, air, and water quality and temperature changes.

David Pinkerton, a physics teacher at Smoky Hill High School in Aurora, Colorado, describes student design projects that illustrate physics principles. Although he lectures periodically as an efficient way to prepare students for problem solving, Pinkerton says, "Cookbook experiments from lab manuals that feature a prescribed set of instructions have been eliminated [from my class]...The 'solve a real problem' format requires a lab team to design their experiment." His list of projects includes the design of an inertial nutcracker that uses no levered jaws; a mini-hovercraft judged on how little friction it generates; a video analysis of a simple motion, such as throwing a ball (the video is then used to construct a graph of human movement); a vehicle that operates on Newton's Third Law; and a functional electric motor (built from one C-cell

Technology Education

battery, two button magnets, a soda straw, three straight pins, and sufficient wire and tape) that serves a new purpose, such as slicing a grape or turning on a light.

Some projects demonstrate how students can affect environmental outcomes through design intervention. Barbara van Wicklin's high school students at Fillmore Central School in Allegany County, New York, create devices and strategies for energy conservation. "One team designed a new electric meter which measures pennies rather than kilowatt hours and outputs costs daily on a small calculator in one's kitchen. The students reasoned that when a person observes money being spent, they are encouraged to turn off the lights and conserve energy."

These research study examples are very much in the spirit of the principles outlined in the *National Science Education Standards.* Through design activities, teachers in this study balance their roles as science experts with facilitation of student discovery and invention.

WHEREAS SCIENCE is about understanding the world, technology is about taking action and knowing how to take action upon our physical surroundings (Bottrill 1995, p. 41). While some educators debate the necessity of involving students in the social and cultural implications of technology, it is clear that technology and design education share similar problem solving concerns: performance expectations for proposed solutions; invention of alternative physical form; testing of prototypes; and assessment of outcomes in human as well as mechanical terms.

Recent studies by national and international organizations reveal that technology education is in a state of creative ferment in schools around the world. The United Nations Educational, Scientific, and Cultural Organization (UNESCO) devotes the fifth volume of

The design process, crucial to technology...should integrate well-developed communication skills with critical thinking skills.

TECHNOLOGY EDUCATION IN THE CLASSROOM, 1996, p. 17

areas of curriculum renovation" (Layton 1994, pp. 11-12).

The Organization for Economic Cooperation and Development (OECD) also cites technology as an emerging discipline in its study of teaching innovations in science, mathematics, and technology around the world. Across the globe, the OECD sees a shift "away from set-piece tasks for the acquisition of specific skills and towards generating solutions to real and complex problems (Black and Atkin 1996, p. 36). The OECD description of the learning outcomes of technology education shares much in common with accounts of design-based classrooms.

...{I}t can draw pupils into a different practice of solving human problems and needs. Some of the means are practical and operational, often involving the making of artifacts, but others require thinking about the design of new systems and environments. To achieve high standards, students have to learn several different things: construction skills, identifying needs, developing optimum designs, acquiring and using necessary knowledge from science, from mathematics, and from other disciplines as the problem demands, and evaluating their own and other people's solutions. As a subject, technology can be distinctive by its interdisciplinary character and for its power to develop students' practical capability for tackling complex problems (Black and Atkin 1996, p. 88).

In the United States, the National Center for Improving Science Education (NCISE) published its own study of the subject titled *Technology Education in the Classroom: Understanding the Designed World*. The international study team assembled by Center director Senta Raizen finds that most member nations in the OECD are ahead of the United States in introducing technology across all grade levels. Rather than "coherent, carefully planned sequences of technology education from kindergarten through twelfth grade," the NCISE reports that American schools more often present the subject "in bits and pieces—an isolated project here, a replacement unit there, or at best, a single year-long course that provides in-depth treatment of a few topics, but offers no continuity or sequence from one year to the next" (Raizen, Sellwood, Todd, and Vickers 1995, p. 3).

One reason for this disjointed practice, according to the Center, is that technology education, unlike other academic disciplines, has not articulated a clear path of intellectual progression from kindergarten through advanced university studies. The International Technology Education Association (ITEA), with funding from the National

its series on *Innovations in Science and Technology Education* to an exploration of this phenomenon. British educator and series editor David Layton notes that whether countries are developing or industrialized, "the case for technology as a component of general education is under examination and is impelling specific curriculum innovations... Also, what is incontestable is the energy and vitality of the field. It has emerged as one of the most exciting, challenging and potentially significant

Science Foundation and the National Aeronautics and Space Administration, recently launched the *Technology for All Americans Project* to develop national voluntary standards, much like those for other school subjects. In 1996, the project released *The Rationale and Structure for the Study of Technology,* which sets forth the field's "knowledge base" (International Technology Education Association 1996).

NCISE finds classrooms in which a craft-based approach emphasizes psychomotor skills in manipulation of traditional materials such as wood, metal, and textiles. Students make products according to prescribed designs, rather than based on their own analysis, methods, and evaluation. Even in classrooms sporting the latest high-tech equipment, instruction may limit students to the mastery of operational skills rather than cultivate critical thought. Elsewhere, teachers emphasize theoretical understanding of technological processes to the exclusion of practical applications where students test understanding and press the technology envelope through new designs.

To illustrate how well-designed technology education integrates various disciplines, the authors present the example of a semester-long junior high school activity in which students design a toy glider suitable for 10-year-old children and the systems for assembling, packaging, and marketing it.

In science, students explore how some plants and animals glide and the strength-to-weight relationships of different materials. In mathematics they examine the geometry of different wing and fuselage configurations; measure the flight lengths, times, and trajectories; and calculate the cost of materials needed for their product and its packaging. They also must consider the costs associated with purchasing raw materials, manufacturing, distribution, and advertising. The packaging must protect the product and function as part of a marketing strategy. The class looks at past attempts at human flight and documents its own design process in a portfolio. A team of four teachers collaborates on facilitation for this project (Raizen et al. 1995, pp. 78-81).

One place where a comprehensive approach to technology education is particularly evident is Willamette Primary School, in West Linn, Oregon. Examples from the school appear throughout this book. All teachers at Willamette understand and integrate both the design process and technology across all subject areas. Susan Dunn, who wrote *Design Technology: Children's Engineering* with Rob Larson, served as the school's first instructional coordinator. In their book, Dunn and Larson contrast the design-rich experiences of children in the past with those of young people in today's consumer culture whose play is largely conditioned by toy manufacturers and children's media. There is less opportunity for young people to exercise their own imaginations and realize their vision through their own hands. Dunn and Larson believe design

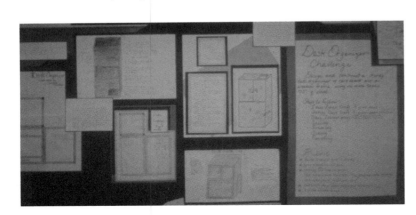

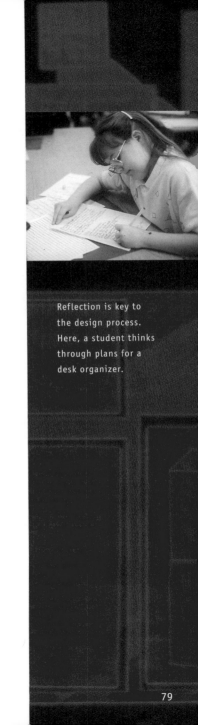

Reflection is key to the design process. Here, a student thinks through plans for a desk organizer.

I feel that when a student designs and tests a system personally, the learning is intrinsic and there is ownership. Children are full of brilliant ideas. They just need an environment to create and express themselves... I would be frustrated as an educator if design were not a part of how I teach.

STEVE BRADY, 7-8th grade technology teacher, Burnsville, MN

technology can reacquaint children with these natural human capabilities.

At Dranesville Elementary School in Herndon, Virginia, teacher Stephen Knobloch asks students to construct a method by which they can move a pound of sand one foot vertically off the ground. Linked to a social studies unit on pyramids in ancient Egypt, this technology project investigates pneumatics, simple machines, hydraulics, and gravity. In other Dranesville classes, students develop design and technology solutions for a great variety of problems: how to keep geese from using the ponds and walking on the greens at a local golf course; how to transport Little Red Riding Hood's cookies to Grandmother's house via a "wolf-proof container"; and how to get three Billy Goats Gruff safely across a river to greener pastures on the other side.

TIES Magazine and Project UPDATE, both based at The College of New Jersey (formerly Trenton State College) encourage the integration of design and technology across the K-8 curriculum. *TIES Magazine* (Technology Innovation and Entrepreneurship for Students) regularly features examples of design and technology from schools in the United States and abroad. Project UPDATE (Upgrading Practice through Design and Technology/Engineering Education) is a multi-year effort in

K-8 teacher training and curriculum development. Funded by the National Science Foundation, the project works with pilot schools from New York to Virginia, using design problem-solving methods as a means of integrating math, science, and technology education.

In its first phase, Project UPDATE helps teachers design Contextual Learning Units (CLUs) integrating the three primary subjects with others through four themes: travel, the built environment, events, and amazing machines. One teacher developed a number of units around the theme of *A Sailing Trip to China.* She developed a topic web that included map making and reading; measuring distances and calculating time; investigating specific gravity and relative density, buoyancy, tidal energy, and wave energy; and appreciating the art, music, and culture of China. Design and technology opportunities arise throughout this journey to China, from making and testing sailboats to designing efficient travel gear, to making and flying dragon kites. All emphasize the design process (Project UPDATE 1996, pp. 2-9).

Exemplifying the new breed of technology teachers, Stephen Scanlon of Marlton, New Jersey admits design

has transformed his teaching and his students' learning.

For the first fourteen years of my teaching career I taught industrial arts education. I emphasized materials and processes. Design? Build the plastic and wood, three-tiered candy dish exactly like the model in class and you will receive an A. For fourteen years!! Now? Active learning by design is the class and what we teach and learn. Whether in sixth, seventh, or eighth grade, students are taught through activities that require design... The biggest change in my teaching and classroom environment has been the excitement that my students bring to class with them. No longer are they confined to producing projects that are designed by someone else with results that are very predictable.

Scanlon introduces his 6th grade students to design in the context of exploring the role of invention and innovation in our society. What motivates people to "pursue a better mousetrap"? How do analyzing problems and achieving design solutions depend upon "thinking differently"?

In 7th grade, Scanlon's students form the 2M Design and Package Company, collaborating with students in Susan Bishop's food, nutrition, and consumer studies class to develop a new snack food and design the packaging and marketing for it.

In the 8th grade control technology class, Scanlon's students demonstrate their knowledge of electronics, pneumatics, robotics, and other subjects by designing conveyor systems, burglar alarms, and other devices. In the advanced science and technology course, students build machines to illustrate the application of scientific principles.

Scanlon acknowledges that open-ended problem solving initially frustrates some students. Gradually, however, "students come to understand that responsibility for learning is now directed back to them. This atmosphere lends itself to a more positive response from all the different types of students within a class ... Ultimately when students identify a problem on their own and solve that problem on their own, they realize that they can control their world."

Crossing the threshold into high schools, one finds fewer occasions that motivate teachers to work in an interdisciplinary way. Given that college and career decisions loom on the horizon for students, many teachers emphasize training in specific technologies. Design in these classrooms is more prescriptive and likely to focus on figuring out internal mechanics rather than addressing the interface between technology and users.

Nevertheless, even some high school technology teachers are taking a second look at the benefits of integrating designerly thinking more firmly into their curricula. In some cases, they follow the lead of colleagues in other countries. In other instances, they respond to the increasing importance business assigns to design as a competitive strategy in the global marketplace. As more elementary and middle schools introduce technology within the context of the design process, many high school teachers also discover that their students have expectations to continue working from a design perspective.

Working in design teams, Gary Finke's students at Oak Harbor High School in Oak Harbor, Ohio, tackle projects in architecture, photography, and computer-automated manufacturing. In one class, students designed a firehouse needed in nearby Toledo; in another, they designed and built part of a manufacturing plant that moves materials using robotics and an automated assembly line. Finke looks to industry for inspiration and seeks out books, videotapes, and workshops that reveal how teams of designers and engineers work together in real-world settings. Finke's most motivated

Middle school students discuss airplane design at a "Dare to Fly" event sponsored by the East Orange and Hasbrouck Heights, New Jersey, school districts.

architecture
robotics
pneumatics
electronics

students frequently devote free periods and after-school hours to their projects.

In Philadelphia, Lincoln High School teachers Donald Testa and Nick Zecca teach design and technology to 9th graders as part of Acatech, a new charter school-within-a-school emphasizing academics applied to technology. Responding to this mandate, the teachers use design methods to update and modify previous industrial and vocational offerings. Having learned about British methods through inservice courses at Drexel University, Testa and Zecca use a variety of design briefs to address student aspirations and society's needs. Students design and make child-safe toys with moving parts, build and test structures for their load-bearing capacity, and create logos and monograms.

In Newark, Delaware, Paul Devine teaches technology classes for 9th through 12th grade students at Glasgow High School. The curriculum has three clusters: communications technology, physical technology, and bio-related technology. Whatever the grade or cluster, Devine encourages his students to explore the multiple dimensions of contexts for which they create design solutions. For example, in redesigning a 1922 row house for a family of three in Wilmington, Delaware, Devine asks students not only to accommodate contemporary needs and technology, but to consider designs of the past, how they are a reflection of their time, and how today's buildings can use concepts from the past in their design. In product development assignments, Devine prompts students to weigh the ecological and ethical implications of the ways in which they acquire and process raw materials and dispose of manufacturing byproducts and finished products.

Devine searches for ways to link his courses with other disciplines. Upon learning that the Smithsonian Institution in Washington planned to dispose of a model simulating a fresh water marsh, he obtained it for the school, then worked with math, science, and environmental education teachers to develop related curricula. The technology students designed modifications to the model to complement student experiments.

Environmental Education

DURING THE PAST 30 years, American educators have broadened the initial emphasis in environmental education from a concern for air and water quality to a more comprehensive approach to teaching about ecosystems. Responding to the flurry of energy conservation efforts during the oil crisis of the 1970s, educators began to pay more attention to the impact of the built world on the natural environment. More recently, interest in sustainable development has encouraged yet another transformation in environmental education, stimulating renewed interest in ways to educate students about interrelated systems at all levels.

A watershed event in changing perspectives on environmental education was the United Nations' Conference on Environment and Development, held in Rio de Janeiro in 1992. Popularly known as the Earth Summit, it forged the critical link between education and our planet's ability to sustain an ever-burgeoning population. Looking at a 40-year window of opportunity before the trajectories of resource depletion and population explosion lead to widespread calamities, the conference called upon all nations to develop plans for transforming their social, economic, and governmental practices.

In June 1993, the White House established the President's Council on

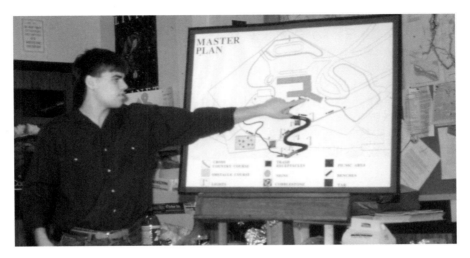

Sustainable Development—consisting of 25 leaders in government, industry, education, and environmental advocacy—to create a national action strategy for sustainable development. Central to the recommendations in the Council's 1996 report is the provision of high-quality education that enables young people "to understand the interdependence of economic prosperity, environmental quality, and social equity—and prepares them to take actions that support all three" (President's Council on Sustainable Development 1996, p. vi).

The Council emphasizes that education for sustainability should not be a new subject grafted onto an already busy school curriculum but a fundamental way of informing all teaching and learning. Design perspectives shape understanding of broad issues of sustainability and are necessary to transform patterns of consumption, business practices, and environmental planning.

The principles underlying education for sustainability include, but are not limited to, strong core academics, understanding the relationships between disciplines, systems thinking, lifelong learning, hands-on experiential learning, community-based learning, technology, partnerships, family involvement, and personal responsibility (President's Council on Sustainable Development 1996, p. 70).

As examples in this book reveal, some innovative teachers already engage students in such community-based

Design perspectives are necessary to transform patterns of environmental planning. With help from the KIDS Consortium, students at Edward Little High School in Auburn, Maine, created a recreational master plan for their campus and its adjacent woods and then won school board and city council approval for the plan.

learning experiences, drawing upon several disciplines in the curriculum. These teachers admit, however, that they often have to piece together such holistic instruction, learning about interdisciplinary, design-based methods through their own reading, outside professionals, and the occasional, relevant inservice opportunity.

Recent reports on the state of environmental education confirm this testimony from the field. *Education for Sustainability: An Agenda for Action* makes a series of recommendations for greater integration of information about sustainability in formal and non-formal education. "Discipline-oriented educational processes," however, present obstacles to an interdisciplinary approach. Likewise, schools must overcome "insufficient professional

preparation for teaching the core content of sustainability issues" (Education for Sustainability Working Group 1996, p. 8). Agenda for Action also finds widespread variation in state policies supporting the inclusion of environmental education in the curriculum and in teacher training.

Most new teachers graduate from teacher preparation institutions with limited knowledge of education for sustainability and ways that it can be incorporated into their teaching…{M}ost teacher preparation programs have not incorporated the necessary content and methods. In fact, most university professors who offer core courses in educational methodology have not themselves had the preparation necessary to infuse sustainability concepts into their courses and the internships they oversee (Education for Sustainability Working Group 1996, p. 15).

Many of the inservice courses and instructional materials available to elementary and secondary school teachers originate in public agencies and nonprofit organizations concerned with various aspects of natural resource protection. Responding to a survey undertaken by the National Consortium on Environmental Education and Training, teachers report that such inservice opportunities are often strong in content but weak in pedagogical

strategies. Similarly, teachers find that much of the material for classroom use raises awareness of basic ecological principles but does not help them to strengthen students' skill in analyzing resource management alternatives and exploring other aspects of the human-environment relationship (Wade 1994).

In its recent report to Congress, the National Environmental Education Advisory Council decries the limited, topical focus of many environmental curricula and advocates "a more balanced menu of materials and programs that emphasize skill development and action, and that stress the interdisciplinary nature of environmental issues" (National Environmental Education Advisory Council 1996, p. 17). The Council's guidelines for exemplary practice call for teachers to help students explore the environment in its totality, even to the point of examining the environmental aspects of plans for development and growth.

From teacher education to curriculum materials, leaders in environmental education are calling for a paradigm shift toward a more comprehensive understanding of the environment, one that encompasses human needs as well as natural resource issues. This requires a multidisciplinary approach, for as one recent study points out, "sustainability is best understood by exploring the

intersections of a number of different dimensions, such as the interaction of social, political, cultural, economic, and ecological perspectives" (Gabriel 1996, p. 22). It calls on environmental educators to develop a "systems thinking pedagogy" to ensure this holistic approach.

As educators develop this new pedagogy, they discover that design lies at the intersections of all these dimensions. Learning about the design of products, buildings, landscapes, and communities; investigating their impact on natural resources; and creating new sustainable solutions to today's problems are ways that teachers can help students develop the knowledge and skills needed for a more balanced world.

Under the auspices of the North American Association for Environmental Education, a national multidisciplinary committee is preparing voluntary standards for the field that reflect the paradigm shift described above. The guidelines call for consideration of the social, economic, political, technological, cultural, historical, moral, and aesthetic aspects of environmental issues as well as their biological and physical dimensions. Citing content standards published to date in the natural sciences, social sciences, and humanities, the guidelines show that environment education offers numerous opportunities to meet curricular requirements in those fields by encouraging students to draw

upon knowledge from many other disciplines (North American Association for Environmental Education 1997, pp. 4-5).

In New Jersey, combining the study of built and natural environments is a way to link suburban and inner city schools, as well as various academic subjects. Paul Inderbitzen, head of the American Re-Insurance Company, put together a coalition of public, private, and non-profit partners to sponsor BEES, Inc. (Building Environmental Education Solutions). Its goal is to help schools develop hands-on, in-depth investigations of local environmental problems in a manner that models the complex decision making involved in solving them. By meeting on site and in the classroom with a variety of stakeholders (residents, environmentalists, developers, legislators, city planners, remediators, and others), students come to appreciate the intersecting interests in a particular issue.

During the 1994-1995 school year, BEES brought together students and teachers from Trenton Central High School, Hunterdon Central Regional High School, the private Hun School, and Granville Academy, an afterschool program for disadvantaged youth. The schools worked together to analyze what might be done to reclaim an abandoned industrial site in Trenton for the residential area surrounding it.

The future is not some place we are going to, it is one we are creating. The paths to it are not found, but made, and the making of these pathways changes both the maker and the destination.

UNESCO, *"Qualities Required of Education Today to Meet Foreseeable Demands in theTwenty-first Century,"* 1989, p. 9.

The 60 participating students learned about techniques for testing, washing, and removing contaminated soil. After interviewing neighbors concerning their desires, the students worked with urban planner Tony Nelessen to develop models showing how compatible housing and the necessary public infrastructure could be reintroduced on the site.

The following year, BEES linked students and teachers at inner-city Camden High School with their counterparts at suburban Cherry Hill West to study a former factory site in South Camden designated by the state for the Superfund clean-up program. This investigation involved 80 students along with biology, chemistry, environ-mental science, English, social studies, art, and business teachers. The entire group participated in site visits and meetings with outside specialists, while smaller teams investigated site history, health effects, soil testing, community opinion, government policies and actions, and site redevelopment feasibility and design.

Over the course of the school year, the teams studied the effects of different forms of radiation, conducted tests around the perimeter of the Camden site, and learned about the larger ecological context of the Delaware estuary. Because exploring the issue of environmental justice was a particular objective of the project, the students also interviewed neighborhood residents and toured two other facilities located within 10 blocks of the contaminated site, the county's principal sewage treatment plant, and a major waste-to-energy cogeneration plant.

As the final phase of the project, the students worked with an environmental consultant and the city planner to analyze the feasibility of redeveloping the contaminated site. After estimating the cost of clean-up necessary to proceed with any option, they examined 10 alternatives in terms of accessibility, construction cost, profitability, number of people served, and compatibility with the surrounding neighborhood. The alternatives included low-income housing, school, park, recreation center, gym, skating rink, shopping center, restaurant, movie theater complex, and motel.

For teachers and students alike, participation in these complex investigations of everyday problems is enlightening. "Working on the feasibility committee," says Camden student Bernadette Gray, "made me realize how much work goes into making decisions and determining what to do next." Hun School environmental studies teacher Colleen Balch sums up the long-term benefits:

After these experiences, the students will never be able to look at an environmental problem in a simplistic way again.... The students have gained an understanding that our society is very complex, and they now have a knowledge of the tangled paths they have to walk to reach solutions for such multifaceted problems. Hopefully, they are on the path to feeling empowered to make changes (Building Environmental Education Solutions, Inc. 1996).

Far to the south, the entire 11th grade at Paramount High School in Boligee, Alabama, conducted a year-long environmental investigation through the lens of an architectural challenge: to design a waste treatment facility and environmental education center on the banks of the Tombigbee River. A four-person team of math, science, social studies, and language arts teachers

developed this rich problem statement with help from Ventures in Education, a New York-based organization that assists schools in developing student-centered, constructivist methods of instruction. The Paramount team attended Venture's inservice workshops and worked closely with its Architectural Youth Program, developed by Marc Sokol.

The teachers challenged the 65 students to work together as a design firm, analyzing the social, economic, regulatory, and environmental aspects of the facility and devising their own architectural plans for it. Throughout the year-long process, Brenda Peters, from Auburn University's College of Architecture, Design, and Construction helped students develop skills in drawing, modeling, and constructive criticism of their design ideas.

In science class, the students analyzed different solid waste processes with the assistance of an environmental

scientist from the state's Department of Environmental Management. With the help of a geologist from the University of West Alabama, they then examined the geology, hydrology, topography, and soil composition of the proposed site. In English class, they practiced writing research abstracts and formal reports. In math, they calculated the amount of household waste generated in Greene County and determined that the proposed facility must also treat waste from two additional counties to be profitable.

In developing their design, the students had to determine the space and equipment needs of waste management technology and anticipate the needs of workers at the facility, staff at the environmental education center, and visitors. They surveyed residents in the community concerning their attitudes and interests in environmental education. At the end of the year, the students presented a thorough review of all issues, together with site plans, architectural drawings, and three-dimensional models. So impressed was school superintendent Joseph Dantzler, that he invited the students to present their work to the Greene County Board of Education and representatives from the state Department of Education.

For student June Weston, one of the most valuable benefits of the project

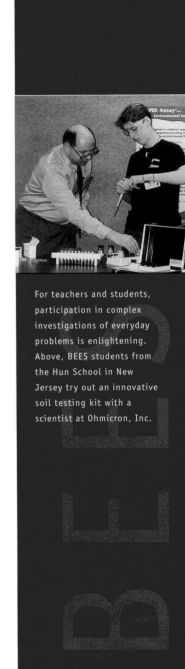

For teachers and students, participation in complex investigations of everyday problems is enlightening. Above, BEES students from the Hun School in New Jersey try out an innovative soil testing kit with a scientist at Ohmicron, Inc.

was "learning not to be intimidated by complex problems, but how to break them down and tackle the various parts in order." For their part, social studies teacher Nancy Cole and her colleagues are convinced of the value of this inter-disciplinary approach for meeting the state's curricular objectives. With a new team of 11th grade students they tackled the design of a comprehensive high school for the county.

It is clear from these examples in social studies, language arts, mathematics, science, technology, and environmental education that teachers find the use of design in their classrooms an effective means for delivering mandated discipline-based curricula. No teachers in the research study expressed concern that design activities displace required content. Instead, all voiced belief that through design they better achieve learning objectives in their respective fields. In most cases, the added benefit of design activities is to connect disciplinary study to larger contexts.

References

American Association for the Advancement of Science, Project 2061. (1989). *Science for All Americans*. New York: Oxford University Press.

American Association for the Advancement of Science, Project 2061. (1993). *Benchmarks for Science Literacy*. New York: Oxford University Press.

Black, P. and Atkin, J.M. (1996). *Changing the Subject: Innovations in Science, Mathematics, and Technology Education*. New York: Routledge, with the Organization for Economic Cooperation and Development (OECD) in Paris, France.

Bottrill, P. (1995). *Designing and Learning in the Elementary School*. Reston, Virginia: International Technology Association.

Building Environmental Education Solutions, Inc. (1996). *BEES Program Brochure*. Princeton, New Jersey: BEES, Inc.

Center for Civic Education. (1994). *National Standards for Civics and Government*. Calabasas, California: Center for Civic Education.

Dunn, S., and Larson, R. (1990). *Design Technology: Children's Engineering*. Bristol, Pennsylvania: The Falmer Press.

Education for Sustainability Working Group. (1996). *Education for Sustainability: An Agenda for Action*. Washington, D.C.: President's Council on Sustainable Development.

Education Update. (January 1997). "It's All In the Videotape." p. 3. Alexandria, Virginia: Association for Supervision and Curriculum Development.

Gabriel, N. (1996). *Teach Our Teachers Well: Strategies to Integrate Environmental Education into Teacher Education Programs*. Boston, Massachusetts: Second Nature.

Geography Education Standards Project. (1994). *Geography for Life: National Geography Standards*. Washington, D.C.: National Geographic Research and Exploration.

International Reading Association and the National Council of Teachers of English. (1996). *Standards for the English Language Arts*. Newark, Delaware: IRA and Urbana, Illinois: NCTE.

International Technology Education Association. (1996). *The Rationale and Structure for the Study of Technology*. Washington, D.C.: ITEA.

Joyce, M. (1994). *Of Two Minds: Hypertext Pedagogy and Poetics*. Ann Arbor, Michigan: University of Michigan Press.

Layton, D., ed. (1994). *Innovations in Science and Technology Education*. Paris, France: United Nations Educational, Scientific, and Cultural Organization (UNESCO).

National Council of Teachers of English and International Reading Association. (1996). *Standards for English Language Arts*. Urbana, Illinois and Newark, Delaware: NCTE and IRA.

National Council of Teachers of Mathematics. (1989). *Curriculum and Evaluation Standards for School Mathematics*. Reston, Virginia: NCTM.

National Environmental Education Advisory Council. (1996). *Report Assessing Environmental Education in the United States and Implementation of the National Environmental Education Act of 1990*. Washington, D.C.: Environmental Protection Agency.

The National Research Council, National Academy of Sciences. (1996). *National Science Education Standards*. Washington, D.C.: National Academy Press.

National Science Teachers Association. (1992). *Scope, Sequence, and Coordination of Secondary School Science, Volume I. The Content Core: A Guide for Curriculum Developers*. Washington, D.C.: NSTA.

North American Association for Environmental Education. (draft 1997). *Environmental Education Guidelines for Excellence: What School-Age Learners Should Know and Be Able To Do*. Washington, D.C.: NAAEE.

President's Council on Sustainable Development. (1996). *Sustainable America: A New Consensus for Prosperity, Opportunity, and a Healthy Environment for the Future*. Washington, D.C.: President's Council on Sustainable Development.

Project UPDATE. (1996). *Contextual Learning Unit (CLU) and Support Materials*. Trenton, New Jersey: The College of New Jersey, Department of Technological Studies.

Raizen, S.A., Sellwood, P., Todd, R.D., and Vickers, M. (1995). *Technology Education in the Classroom: Understanding the Designed World*. San Francisco, California: Jossey-Bass Publishers, Inc.

Technology for All Americans Project. (1996). *Technology for All Americans: A Rationale and Structure for the Study of Technology*. Reston, Virginia: International Technology Association.

Wade, K. (1994). *National Survey of Environmental Education Teacher Inservice Education*. Ann Arbor, Michigan: Regents of the University of Michigan.

5
OPPORTUNITIES AND
Challenges for Schools

Researchers have found that even very young children engage in complex thinking and problem-solving. For this reason, educators talk less today about whether the child is ready for school and more about whether the school is ready for the child.

THE HOLMES GROUP,
Tomorrow's Schools of Education, 1995, p. 29

When examined within the broader context of a school or district, design-based learning presents new ways for realizing long-term goals and learning outcomes. In a discussion of school- and district-level implementation of design strategies, it is easy to focus on physical obstacles to systemwide adoption. However, the strength of a design approach to curriculum and instruction lies in its ability to provide a new construct for educational reform and to challenge long-held practices that stand in the way of achieving significant progress in improving schools for children.

The research for this book reveals key issues surrounding support, expansion, and maintenance of design-based curricula. The issues come from the experiences of students, teachers, and administrators who use design-based learning in their classrooms and schools. They are:

- use of resources in schools,

- teacher education and support, and

- beliefs and assumptions about students, teachers, schools, and community.

It is important to note that these issues are not unique to using design in the classroom. They are the same issues raised by those calling for educational reform and by researchers examining the effectiveness of curriculum, instruction, and the business of schools.

© SUSIE FITZHUGH

The traditional school structure does not allow this very natural process.

RESOURCE ALLOCATION, including time and space, has long been a focus of educational reform. There is ample evidence that the structure of the school day and the design of classrooms in which learning takes place affect student achievement, just as they affect the productivity and quality of adult achievement in the workplace.

Time

Many teachers report that teaching through design runs counter to the ways in which schools organize the school day. The most common observation is the mismatch between the time needed to tackle rich, complex problems and the regular intervals at which children must change classes or shift attention to other subjects. The process of designing, teachers point out, requires varying amounts of time for planning, research, execution, and reflection. For some activities, 45- to 55-minute class periods are sufficient; for others, they are woefully inadequate. Teachers note that without latitude to change daily schedules, the flow of the design process is interrupted and some of the potential strength of learning activities diminishes.

Teachers in self-contained classrooms, as in many elementary schools, or in cross-disciplinary teams, where teachers share adjacent class periods with the same group of students, report fewer

problems with external time constraints. They can extend or contract assigned time periods to adapt to the demands of learning activities. However, in school settings where the academic day is tightly organized into regular periods of time and students work with many teachers who do not function as a team, the conflict between schedules and the type of learning implicit in design activity is more striking.

For example, Smoky Hill High School physics teacher David Pinkerton negotiates with students and other teachers to allow his class to participate in hour-long assessments of their Rube Goldberg machines. Students must seek permission to miss and then make up time in other classes as they deliver their elaborate projects to school, set them up, and pretest them in preparation for Pinkerton's assessment of each team's work. Pinkerton says, "Design [projects] require time to make a prototype, see how it behaves, and adjust it, based on the interactions. The traditional school structure does not allow this very natural process."

Administrators also acknowledge the challenge. Stanley Hestings, vice principal at Smoky Hill High School, observes, "Discrete course periods like those in high schools and middle schools make it difficult to accommodate irregular or uneven requests for extended periods of time to undertake and complete a design task. To do it, we need to rethink the way the whole school is organized. You see, with a schedule like ours, changes like that can affect a dozen other teachers."

The control teachers exercise over time allocation within their classrooms is also a factor in the use of design in the curriculum. Teachers report that initially they have difficulty in gauging how long it will take students to complete a project. With experience, they gain a better sense of how long some projects require. However, there are no guarantees. A concept that one group of students masters in two days could take a week with another group of children. Within the same class, students require differing amounts of time to complete an assignment. While traditional classroom activities often mask the varying rates at which children learn, design activities make them visible and allow the teacher to address student problems at an early stage in their learning tasks.

The second area of concern about available time is teacher planning and coordination of design activities. Virtually all school reform efforts involving cross-disciplinary instruction discover that the traditional school schedule makes little provision for teachers' joint planning, coordination

of instruction, and reflection. Based on regular class periods, the traditional school schedule inserts planning time in individual teachers' schedules without regard for teamwork. Team-based approaches to using design in the classroom suffer from the same inflexible time structure that plagues any teaching team. It is fair to conclude that students do not experience a truly integrated educational program when their teachers cannot plan together and coordinate instruction during the school day.

Furthermore, it is not feasible for teachers to complete joint planning for the entire school year in the two or three inservice days before the start of school. The teachers in this study claim planning for design activities and curriculum must be ongoing and responsive to issues and demands that arise throughout the year.

In several of the site-visit schools, such as Willamette Primary School and Dranesville Elementary School, administrators attempt

to schedule joint teacher planning time within each school day. Principal Madeline Brennan at the Dyker Heights Intermediate School recognized this need upon initiating the design-based program in her school: "A common preparation period was provided so that teachers could discuss options for multidisciplinary units of study and to identify those subjects which could be aligned to benefit the students' thinking." At many other schools, however, most teams of teachers using design in their classrooms report voluntarily extending their work day to meet or talk on the phone with fellow teachers from their team.

A teacher at Beaver Acres Elementary School in Beaverton, Oregon, takes time to discuss a student's design for corn husk dolls.

Space

The second challenge in the use of
resources concerns the organization
and control of physical space. Demands
for larger, alternately configured, or
otherwise flexible classroom space are
common among teachers who use
design activities in their curriculum.
Generally, the traditional classroom
with rows of individual desks better
accommodates janitors than it does
teachers and learners.

Many teachers in this study cite
appropriate furniture and classroom
space as central to the success of design
projects. Tables around which groups
of students cluster are preferable to
individual desks. In schools where

design and technology are a focus,
tables are common features in most
classrooms, and teachers configure
them differently for each activity.

Without question, space for storage,
building, and presentation plays a key
role in design experiences, as it does
in any active, project-based learning.
Design-based classrooms are distin-
guished by the sheer volume of material
that adorns walls; covers floors, tables,
and desks; and spills into hallways. Many
projects are three-dimensional and made
of fragile materials requiring special
storage. These projects can easily over-
whelm typical classroom closets and
cupboards, as well as bulletin boards,
notebooks, and file folders designed for
more traditional products of education.

Reallocation of Resources

The degree of support for design varied
widely among the schools in this study.
In some cases, districts allocate additional resources, beyond those provided
for traditional schools, to support
design-based instruction. These resources
may include teaching and professional
staff, materials, equipment, and technological support. At Dranesville
Elementary School and Willamette
Primary School, funding for technology
and instruction coordinators initially
was part of the overall school budgets.
At Tippecanoe Elementary School for

the Humanities, a full-time art specialist supports classroom design activities,
and a coordinator manages and supports
the overall program. These coordinators do not have classroom teaching
responsibility and devote their time
exclusively to curriculum and inservice
coaching of teachers. Their presence
provides school-and system-level support that sustains programs through
changes in classroom teachers and
institutional policies. They also provide a liaison between the school or the
classroom and administration, reporting on achievements and obstacles to
effective instruction.

Several schools in this study establish separate budget lines to finance
design activities. Computer software
and hardware purchases are frequent
expenditures. More typically, however,
teachers report that they scavenge for
funds to supplement their budgets and
make use of found or donated materials. It was clear from our site visits that
for many activities teachers employ
inexpensive materials and that finding
things and putting them to a new use
are part of the learning process for
children. It was also evident that the
teacher who uses design in the classroom is resourceful; none said he or
she was unable to use a design approach
to teaching because of a lack of expensive equipment.

Teacher Education and Support

MOST OF THE teachers in this study did not gain competencies in design-based teaching and learning through traditional teacher education programs. With few exceptions, the teachers who appear in this study developed expertise in a design approach to teaching in one of four ways:

- through prior work in design, including study for degrees in architecture and graphic design;

- through inservice programs supported by professional societies or other design-related organizations;

- through independent development of new strategies after years of frustration with traditional methods; or

- through coaching in the design process by a designer relative, friend, or instructional coordinator.

Preservice and inservice teacher training are critical to the success of all education reform efforts. Teachers need to exhibit the same competencies as students: an understanding of systems, problem-solving skills, teamwork, proficiency with technology, manipulation of information, and efficient allocation of resources. Traditional approaches to teacher preparation are not oriented toward ensuring that teacher candidates develop these competencies in their professional work. While this has implications for the success of many school reform efforts, it is particularly important for the use of design in the classroom, both as a strategy for teaching and as subject matter.

Sheila McCoy, Dean of the College of Education and Integrative Studies at California State Polytechnic University at Pomona, describes the shift that must take place in teacher education.

Design-based approaches force teachers to really think about what they are doing. For many teachers, it is the first time they are building from the ground up, not from surface material down. Teachers don't generally begin from nothing. They deal with boxes of curriculum materials and prepared content. They want things cut up in neat packages. Teachers in my college-level education classes frequently ask me, "What will be on the exam?" Design forces them to go back and ask themselves why they are trying to do something. It forces them to function as creators and authors, which teachers rarely do without a design education.

David Kennedy, Director of Educational Technology in the Washington State Office of Public Instruction, describes the challenges of changing departments of education and the preservice and inservice preparation of teachers. He believes state administrations and colleges suffer from "hardening of the categories" and "massive territoriality" that work against design and any approaches that encourage integration of subject matter or new ways of thinking.

Sheila McCoy confirms the struggle to insert new approaches in college curricula, citing her own administrative efforts to gain university approval for Doreen Nelson's innovative master's degree program in design and creativity, based on City Building Education.

Students at the Enlightenment School in Waterbury, Connecticut, complete a model of their school.

"Teachers have to develop expertise within their school in order to achieve a long-term commitment; they have to make sure there is the right kind of spirit in the building."

McCoy describes design as "deceptively simple," often disguising its intellectual power in activities that resemble play. McCoy believes people have to see this approach in action or be part of an activity to be convinced that it taps higher-order thinking skills.

Myron Atkin, professor of technology education at Stanford University, goes a step further in talking about the problems of introducing design-based strategies in teacher education. Atkin says, "Schools of education depend on professorial interest in adopting or not adopting new approaches as part of their teacher education curricula." If an education professor's personal interests don't support new approaches, students in that college or university don't learn them. He cites the pervasiveness of science/technology/society courses on U.S. campuses and the study of the social implications of science as much likelier orientations than his own design-based approach to technology education. Atkin also believes, "Most teacher education is geared to state certification. It is the state framework that really guides what is taught.... Western education glorifies the abstract, but concrete action and practical reasoning glorify the species. We have taken this kind of learning out of our education, and it is time to bring it back."

While educators are somewhat divided on how to best achieve reform in teacher education, many agree that inservice workshops are insufficient in creating sustained change in teaching practices. McCoy says, "You're always

Teachers learn design and model-making techniques at a workshop offered by the Salvadori Educational Center on the Built Environment. Teachers take these techniques back to their schools and share them with others, developing their own expertise and building a spirit of collegiality.

confronted with the question of how to deal with groups of people who have different knowledge. You can't even out the experiences in a short period of time."

Leona Schauble, professor of educational psychology in the College of Education at the University of Wisconsin-Madison, also believes that workshops are not the best way to bring about change. Instead, an ongoing, one-to-one relationship between 30-40 teachers and the university's center for mathematics and science education allows Schauble and her colleagues to regularly videotape teachers' work and show them how to author their own projects and curricula.

Susan Dunn, former instructional coordinator at Willamette Primary School, believes some people can learn a design approach through workshops or on their own, but she adds, "They miss the continuing conversation from the college classroom to their schools." Dunn teaches graduate-level courses as an adjunct professor at Lewis and Clark College and has taught graduate courses at the three schools in which she has been an administrator. Many of her teachers enroll in master's degree programs that divide college coursework between satellite classes in their own schools and the Lewis and Clark College campus. Their study includes research, assessment, child development, teaching strategies, and practicum. Dunn says, "Teachers have to develop expertise within their school in order to achieve a long-term commitment; they have to make sure there is the right

kind of spirit in the building. The collegiality with other teachers is as important as the relationship between their graduate study and what they are doing at school. Immersion creates a more supportive environment and makes change a way of life." Dunn also accepts teaching interns from Lewis and Clark College and frequently hires them when they graduate. She calls this a "long-term commitment to building the fabric of the school."

In the design and creativity master's program in education at California State Polytechnic University at Pomona, director and professor Doreen Nelson visits her graduate students' classrooms to observe how teachers reassess traditional strategies and transform their roles as curriculum planners

...to identify **design** as relevant to their teaching and to find sources that provide information in support of design-based curriculum and instruction

and authors of new approaches. Dean Sheila McCoy says, "This process in which the teacher learns to perceive herself or himself as a designer can be scary for some; they have to create this thing, to step into the unknown." She cites Nelson's commitment to go beyond the college classroom as one reason for her teachers' success.

Gail Johnson, Acting Coordinator for Certification and Personnel at the Utah State Office of Education, is more positive about short-term workshops. She observes teachers from Adele Weiler's Building Connections workshops on the built environment. Johnson believes changes in teacher behavior are consistent with statistics from the National Council for Staff Development: 10 percent of the participants are "on board" immediately, while another 60-70 percent come along in time. There is strong evidence that Weiler's concepts and practices become part of the teachers' yearly programs and that they revise their work and often retake the workshops. The State Office of

Education updates teachers with information on new strategies from year to year. Johnson also believes design workshops spark higher retention than other topics. She observes, "Because the workshops are participatory and teachers are actively engaged, the information stays with them."

Jan Norman, chair of the Department of Art and Museum Education at the University of the Arts in Philadelphia, agrees that there is some value in short-term workshops. Norman runs design-based workshops for Pennsylvania teachers from all subject areas. For the most part, her participants are seasoned teachers with long-term commitments to the classroom, not beginners. Norman says, "Most are interested in the problem-solving element and ways of teaching higher levels of thinking." However, Norman admits many teachers implement only a single design project in their annual curriculum. She believes the ability to sustain a design approach to instruction depends on long-term

plans for integrated curriculum and ongoing assessment.

At the University of the Arts, Jan Norman developed courses in design-based instruction for undergraduate and graduate students in collaboration with Charles Burnette, chair of the university's industrial design program. Students who have a strong professional education in design can become certified to teach K-12 students.

Donna Kay Beattie, associate professor of art education at Brigham Young University, shares with Norman an interest in methods through which students enrolled in undergraduate college design programs can acquire the qualifications to teach in K-12 classrooms. Beattie sees differences between her students in design and those engaged in visual arts: "The design majors are characterized by open-mindedness and the ability to approach teaching problems from many directions." The Brigham Young program also requires a design component in the art education curriculum and

offers a design specialization option for art education majors.

Since current university curricula for the preparation of teachers do not include the study of design as subject matter or as a pedagogical strategy, teachers must rely on their own resourcefulness to identify design as relevant to their teaching and to find sources that provide information in support of design-based curriculum and instruction. The lack of recognition of design and design education by university programs and the absence of resources in schools for ongoing teacher education remain serious obstacles to wider adoption of design-based instruction.

Instructional Support and Supervision

The research revealed that instructional and administrative support for the use of design in schools and school districts is uneven. There are a few examples of strong commitment to design by district administrators, but the majority of teachers who use design in their classrooms labor in isolation.

Joel Montero, superintendent of the Novato Unified School District in California, is one of the exceptions. Clearly, Montero understands the benefits of design-based instruction and works to sustain a supportive environment for educators who are

willing to reassess their teaching practices. Montero says,

What education hasn't done well in the past is foster applicative learning. "Design-build" or "design-develop" concepts ask students to apply what they know.... We have several teachers who provide leadership in this approach. What you need is a kernel of interest, then critical mass at any school site, and the work begins to evolve and grow. The district has to be supportive. It doesn't all work perfectly the first time. If you're squeamish, get out of the way. You have to support teachers on the cutting edge.

Montero's experience with teachers who use a design approach also changed his attitudes about who he needs to hire. He looks for teachers who are "noncontrollers" and who are "not afraid of technology." Responding to what he sees as lack of preparation by colleges of education, Montero has developed a three-year "new teacher" training program that focuses on application-based learning. In many cases,

he uses his own teachers as inservice instructors who conduct workshops for their colleagues.

Finally, Montero takes responsibility for providing the community with a picture of success, for translating into action what an educated person needs to know. In doing this, Montero involves the business community through a "business education roundtable" of 40 companies that advise him and his teachers about the likely demands of the workplace in the future.

As Montero demonstrates, to sustain design-based learning and teaching, teachers must have ongoing support from curriculum supervisors and principals. First, because design is inherently interdisciplinary, teachers must receive inservice training and curriculum materials that balance disciplinary with interdisciplinary and cross-disciplinary study. For the most part, secondary schools charge teachers with the responsibility for transmitting discipline-based content. Design-based

To evaluate staff expertise in teaching through design, school administrators must recognize skills developed by the process itself. Here, two teachers from the Open Charter Magnet School examine their students' city-building process.

strategies must equally address the achievement of specific disciplinary competencies while showing applications in larger interdisciplinary and cross-disciplinary contexts. Any strategy that fails to achieve some level of competency in discipline-based issues is unlikely to receive sustained administrative support in most school systems. Teachers require training in curriculum development and instruction to balance these issues.

Second, the successful use of design in classrooms demands that curriculum supervisors be equally knowledgeable in design so that planning, supervision of instruction, resource allocation, and assessment of teachers mirror what is going on in the classroom. Most curriculum specialists who support the use of design in classrooms gained their interests and expertise through the same informal channels as teachers. Some teachers express concern over the lack of informed specialists who can act as teacher resources and function as advocates for innovative teaching in their districts.

Research indicated that courses in instructional methods, curriculum development, and assessment are appropriate venues for the introduction of new strategies that have their basis in design. Likewise, university laboratory schools are logical sites for experimentation and research in the application

of new methods to classrooms. Such efforts are likely to foster teacher and curriculum specialist comfort with the design process and cultivate the confidence necessary for broader adoption of design-based methods.

Third, the study indicated greater teacher success in schools where administrators support development of teacher teams and bring beginners in design-based approaches to higher levels of comfort with methods used by more experienced coworkers. These administrators recognize the need to construct schoolwide systems for collaboration and renewal of expertise; teachers cannot create these conditions on their own while managing the demands of the normal school day.

While other approaches to education reform share this need for support, evidence from several schools suggests that success is more likely when there is strong support from administration. Willamette Primary School, Dranesville Elementary School, and Dyker Heights Intermediate School have in-school curriculum coordinators for design and technology. As part of the Apple Computer's Vivarium Project, the Los Angeles Open Charter Magnet School provides its design teachers with instruction support through a consultancy with Doreen Nelson using City Building Education. In these

cases, teachers have developed a strong command of design concepts and processes, and they communicate them well to their students.

The use of design as a strategy for teaching and learning also holds promise for teacher assessment and is likely to give teachers useful feedback to guide their practice. Because this type of instruction places the teacher in a role of facilitator, traditional testing of content knowledge and classroom procedures appears insufficient for identifying how successful teachers are. Jim Zinck, chair of the science department at Smoky Hill High School, observes:

Even "new" teacher assessment techniques often do not apply to teaching activities in a design classroom. For example, in visiting a design classroom, I might never observe the teacher engage the entire class at once. Instead, the teacher-as-coach/teacher-as-facilitator/teacher-as-resource roles would result in the instructor moving from student to student or team to team offering advice on strategy, technique, or findings. Some students or teams working independently might never be specifically engaged by the teacher at all {within a normal class period}. If I used the district's {teacher assessment} form, or a {Madeline} Hunter form, I'd have to leave much of it blank because the categories simply don't apply.

disciplinary
interdisciplinary
cross-disciplinary

Beliefs and Assumptions

AS SUGGESTED throughout this book, the use of design in the classroom challenges traditional beliefs and assumptions held by and about schools. Such challenges are inherent in any reform effort, but design-based curricula and instruction, in particular, raise questions about the continuing relevance of three widespread assumptions:

- Discipline-centered instruction is better than interdisciplinary or cross-disciplinary teaching for learning core subjects.

- Design activities are the domain of gifted and talented students in the arts.

- Schools must provide all the resources necessary for learning.

Interdisciplinary Teaching and Learning

For reasons discussed earlier in this book, contemporary reformers extol the value of interdisciplinary and cross-disciplinary teaching. As an inherently interdisciplinary activity, the design process offers an approach for structuring such study. Because design usually involves project-based and situated learning, students who engage in design activities model the work of adults by drawing content and skills from those disciplines necessary to solve a problem. Knowledge must "work" and be useful, not merely be acquired for the purpose of storing facts.

The reflective study of design, in which students think about or comment on design objects or environments and their contexts, is equally cross-disciplinary. In looking at the design of cities, students explore the social, physical, and cultural environments that shape human behavior. Social studies, environmental science, and history play important roles in such investigations. In analyzing visual communication, students "decode" meaning in the relationship between word and image. Such assignments integrate skills in the language arts, art, history, and technology. While active involvement in the design process usually characterizes most design-based learning, these reflective activities are also the foundation for developing discriminating consumers who make critical choices in their adult lives. Because reflection on design frequently addresses systems-level problems, such as communication and the environment, it is also useful in showing students how core subjects relate to each other.

California Polytechnic State University Dean of Education and Integrative Studies Sheila McCoy and others believe design education actually improves teachers' understanding of disciplinary content and, in doing so, prepares them for interdisciplinary

Product designer Vince Foote explains the science inherent in athletic shoe design.

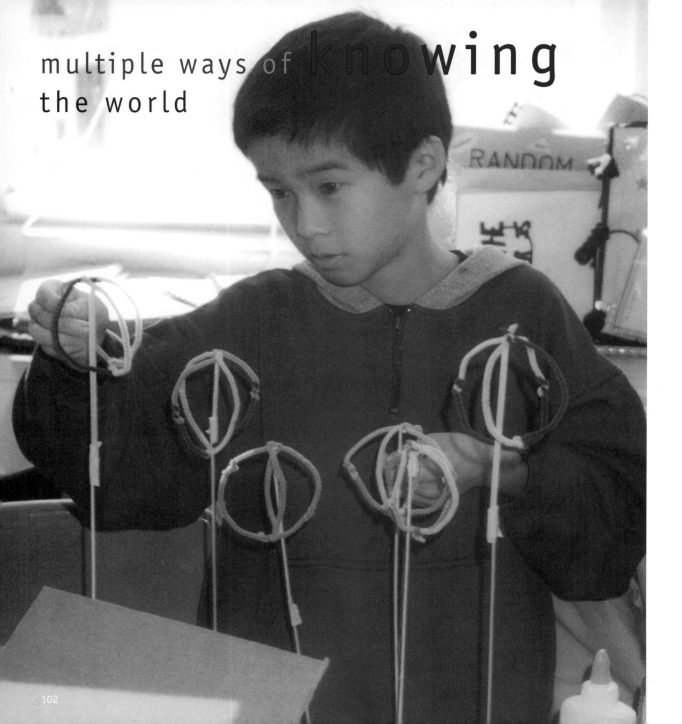

multiple ways of knowing the world

teaching. She says, "Design education shows that ideas have structures, too, and that you can take ideas and make them physical, actual. Design education forces people to go to the inherent structure, to go below the surface, and the more you do this the better your thinking will be. You can only build meaningful connections to your discipline when you look at its structure." David Kennedy concurs: "Design transcends all content areas. It organizes the product of any discipline."

However, interdisciplinary and cross-disciplinary teaching requires planning time and extra effort by teachers. Leona Schauble at the University of Wisconsin's center on math and science education says that in most elementary schools in this country, "there is almost no talking from grade to grade and no sense of what teachers are building upon or toward." In the elementary classrooms documented by this study, teachers prepare new instructional plans that span several subject areas. Art, technology, and science specialists in these schools often coordinate their work with that of classroom teachers to ensure that design activities extend across appropriate time periods during the school day.

Typically, there is less flexibility for innovation in middle and high schools because:

- teachers have less control over the division of the school day;

- school populations are shared by many teachers;

- society expects older students to engage in reflective, rather than active, learning experiences; and

- schools place great emphasis on matching high school discipline-based study to the demands of college.

Research findings of this study support the notion that high schools are less likely to take a design-based approach and to engage in interdisciplinary or cross-disciplinary study. Implementing cross-disciplinary design curricula in the upper grades depends on altering perceptions about the range

© SUSIE FITZHUGH

of ways in which schools achieve disciplinary expertise. Without administrative support to alter traditional practices, such as division of the school day into regular periods of time and the movement of students to new spaces for each subject, there can be little change.

An Approach for All Students

One of the persistent misconceptions about learning is that mastery of basic skills through repetitive learning experiences is a necessary prerequisite for tasks that involve higher-order thinking skills. The result is that the education of younger children, and of older children who perform below grade expectations, often emphasizes repetitive tasks and the acquisition of facts through some prescribed method. One manifestation of this thinking is that while gifted-and-talented programs are frequently the most creative and interesting, classes for "students at risk" function in highly regimented instructional climates.

Several classrooms in this study serve gifted or privileged populations. Some classrooms represent magnet programs or enrichment for academically gifted students. Others are in schools that serve affluent neighborhoods where education is valued highly by the community. In the overwhelming majority of the schools studied, however,

teachers work with a broad range of student abilities representing an array of economic backgrounds. The research also identified classrooms in which design strategies address the needs of less academically able students. In fact, teachers comment that design strategies work better than more traditional methods in engaging students who are reluctant learners.

Stephen Knobloch, a teacher at Dranesville Elementary School, noted, "One of the greatest benefits [of design] for students is providing an opportunity for all students, not just the gifted/talented students, to experience higher-level learning by doing. Many of my most enjoyable teaching experiences have been with learning disabled students who have their greatest success using the design process and then seeing the 'ah ha'."

Stephen Scanlon, a technology education teacher at Marlton Middle School in Marlton, New Jersey, confirms that students with lower performance records have an opportunity to succeed in design experiences. He says, "Design allows the academically frustrated student to realize that 'intelligence' is not confined to textbooks. Design in my classroom allows the spotlight to be turned on students who have formed negative opinions about their role in the educational process."

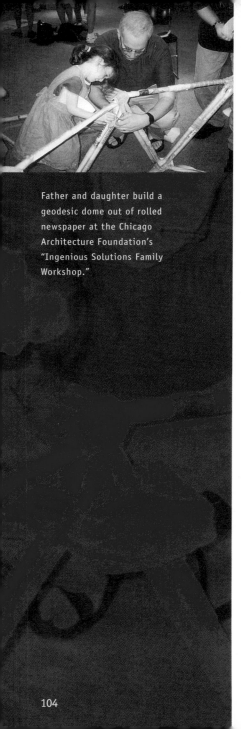

Father and daughter build a geodesic dome out of rolled newspaper at the Chicago Architecture Foundation's "Ingenious Solutions Family Workshop."

Product designer Vince Foote demonstrates the science behind traction for a middle school class in North Carolina.

In at least one instance, at Warren County Middle School in North Carolina, gifted and talented 6th grade students experienced higher frustration with the open-ended nature of their first design project than did their lower-performing classmates. These students were unsettled by the possibility of many "right" answers and by comments that the designs could be improved by exploring alternative viewpoints. Several refused to go to their next class until they could do the activity over again. Steven Scanlon concurs that design instruction can also offer a beneficial, eye-opening experience for students already deemed "successful": "[Design] allows the gifted student who may be frustrated by the regimentation of right, wrong, and one way of doing things to truly explore their talents."

It is also important to note that the research found numerous examples of effective design-based learning and teaching with very young children, including those in kindergarten. Students in the primary grades understand and engage in the design process. Concurring with Howard Gardner and Nigel Cross that there are multiple ways of knowing the world, this study affirms that design strategies provide students of all ages with opportunities to practice and exhibit their mastery of information, resources, and processes through projects that are not part of the traditional curriculum.

Community and Parent Support

One of the major strengths of design-based teaching strategies is that the community becomes integral to instruction. Community partnerships flourish in schools that use design activities in the classroom, with graphic designers, industrial designers, architects, urban planners, contractors, software developers, and others playing active roles in instruction. Through such interaction, students share their perceptions of design issues, build connections between school and work, and expand their understanding, not only of careers in design but of many other adult roles in the community. Because these encounters take

place within the context of solving problems, students gain insight into these varied jobs and come to appreciate how many people shape the built environment. This type of learning does not take place in typical "career day" presentations, where children are simply told about adult work.

Design activities also involve parents in their children's education. Teachers in this study report that parents notice their children's increased interest in school when design activities are introduced into the curriculum. Frequently, assignments spill over into learning activities in the home, which affords parents direct observation of student performance. Teachers also report, however, that parents occasionally require careful explanations of curriculum strategy to see that the school retains a commitment to basic problem-solving skills and that strings of projects add up to more than entertainment. Once informed, these parents usually become strong supporters of design-based approaches to teaching and learning.

Parents and future employers also express concern over assessment. Schools must demonstrate how portfolio assessment and performance-based testing work and what they reveal. While evidence exists supporting the validity and reliability of such evaluation, many people are accustomed to more quantitative indicators of successful learning. Administrators and teachers should not underestimate the effort required to achieve public understanding and acceptance of more comprehensive methods of evaluating what students know and are able to do.

6 CONCLUSIONS AND *Recommendations*

the research for this book suggests that there is great variation in teachers' understanding of the design process and design issues. Many teachers who responded to the questionnaire interpret all active learning as design based. Yet building the Parthenon out of sugar cubes, replicating the Globe Theatre complete with thatched roof, making a computer model of a castle, or constructing an entire village out of cardboard, moss, and twigs are little more than "makework" projects if teachers cannot clarify for students the design thinking that lies behind choosing materials, using technology, and responding to climate and human needs.

Similarly, teachers who don't have a true understanding of the design process cannot adequately coach students to create their own design solutions to a problem, be it imaginary or real. To be able to use the full dimensions of design problem solving to benefit instruction *and* learning, many teachers need a better grounding in the design process so they understand the unique characteristics that distinguish it from other activities.

Some teachers confuse visual products (illustrated book reports, drafted plans for a house) with design problem solving, in which students make critical choices that affect the quality of the environment, efficiency of products, and

effectiveness of communication. While illustrating and drafting are valuable skills that enhance students' work, they rarely go far enough to involve students in making choices about or analyzing important issues related to design or the subject of their investigation.

Many respondents to our questionnaire described projects in which the teacher knows the outcome before students begin the assignment. They also described exercises in terms of prescribed methods for reaching a solution rather than in terms of student inquiry and discovery. These teachers miss the point of the design process. They stifle opportunities to broaden students'

—missing from most
students' experiences is
the notion that design
shapes and reflects the
perception and behavior
of others.

understanding of the subject matter of such investigations and usually assess student performance in terms of how well a resulting product resembles their expectations. To truly use design problem solving, these teachers need ongoing professional critique of their assignments and teaching practices as well as assistance in developing new facilitation skills.

The number of research examples in which design itself is a subject of reflective study are few, indicating teachers' lack of confidence in and education about design as well as limited access to design resources. The teachers who incorporate reflective study of design into social studies and arts curricula generally have prior experience with the subject through formal study or with a colleague or family member who is a design professional. Design issues are not the normal content of teacher preparation.

Even the best classroom examples in our study show a somewhat narrow view of design. In almost all cases, the core design issues are physical, and they center on the study of one or more of the following:

- **the physical conditions to which a design responds,**

- **the physical nature of the environment that design creates,**

- **connection of a culture with only the physical attributes of a designed object, or**

- **the physical activity required to bring form to an idea.**

While these issues are important—and examples show how projects develop design students' thinking skills—missing from most students' experiences is the notion that design shapes and reflects the perception and behavior of others. They are missing out on the idea that designers often make choices based on how they and others want people to think or act.

The definition of "culture" implicit in most of the project examples limits design discussion. In responses to the questionnaire, teachers describe the cultural dimensions of designed objects, environments, or problem solving in terms of ethnic origin or a period in one country's history. For most of the teachers in this study, "culture" equals only the geographical or historical location of the design problem or object of investigation. Rarely do they view culture as shared systems of belief, experience, or circumstances of life. Consequently, few projects penetrate surface definitions of how people identify and represent themselves through their choices about environments, products, and communication— rich territory for discussion and project development.

Most teacher surveys that describe active learning use three-dimensional modeling or construction as primary activities. Although some teacher responses to our questionnaire describe activities in which students make two-dimensional objects, the majority of these represent fine-arts projects, where the primary purpose is self-expression, or technical drafting exercises, where the mental aspects of translating a three- dimensional object into a two-dimensional representation are of lesser importance than the execution of the drawing itself.

Notably absent in the surveys is mention of two-dimensional, graphic communication for the purposes of explaining, informing, or persuading. This is surprising considering the dominance of media in students' lives and the ease of storing these projects in comparison to three-dimensional projects. Teaching students to "encode and decode" visual information is an important aspect of literacy in today's media-rich world and a valuable link to language arts and the analysis of scientific and social studies data.

IT IS EVIDENT that wide adoption of design as a curricular or pedagogical strategy will not happen without serious attention to teacher education and the development of teacher skills, knowledge, and attitudes about design. Such attention must focus on inservice as well as preservice professional development.

Although inservice programs broaden teacher awareness and understanding of design and its use in the classroom, the majority are insufficient in bringing about attitude changes and skills acquisition at levels that prompt permanent change in teaching practices. Research indicates that inservice programs encourage changes in teacher performance in the first year after participation, but the use of new methods declines dramatically in subsequent years. Teachers and researchers attribute this decline to lack of positive reinforcement for their work from school principals, supervisors, and more experienced colleagues.

The Holmes Group, a consortium of 84 research universities, seeks to advance the reform agenda for the education of professionals who work in schools.[1] Its report, titled *Tomorrow's Schools of Education,* cites the weaknesses of continuing education programs for teachers as "their overemphasis on seat-time… [,] their lack of continuity or sustained assistance over time, and their lack of close connection to educational practice as it affects youngsters' learning" (The Holmes Group 1995, pp. 55- 56). This is the culture into which design educators must insert themselves if progress is to be made through inservice and continuing education of teachers in design-based methods.

Currently, few inservice programs promote the use of design in the classroom. Most are led by a handful of university design educators whose primary responsibilities are teaching and research in their respective institutions. These programs range from one-day workshops to summer institutes, with limited opportunity for follow-up once teachers return to their classrooms.

Taking time to appreciate good design work validates the process in the eyes of younger students.

Rarely do programs enroll administrators or a team of teaching professionals from the same school, inhibiting the development of a cadre for in-house reinforcement.

The Holmes Group is equally harsh in its assessment of teacher preservice education in the United States. Included in its criticisms is piecemeal reform that "has proven inadequate because of the web of connections among the system's various parts—curriculum, pedagogy, assessment, texts and materials, and professional development" (The Holmes Group 1995, p. 9). The report goes on to say that, "Students in education programs must experience learning environments where learners search for meaning, appreciate uncertainty, and inquire responsibly so they can recreate such circumstances for their own students" (The Holmes Group 1995, p. 12).

Providing a design-based education for teachers may be more difficult than it appears. On college campuses with design programs, faculty and administrators use already scarce resources to teach small studio classes to future design professionals. Access to design study for majors in nondesign disciplines, such as education, is limited. The studio classes generally involve making design objects with groups of 15-20 students in highly specialized work environments and vertical course structures that require extensive prerequisite study. Education majors rarely compete successfully for registration in such classes. Clearly, design professors interested in broader application of their pedagogical approach should work with education professors to develop courses for teachers that illustrate the design process and its connections to teaching.

While it is unlikely that expensive studio-based instruction will be offered to help reform teacher education, lecture courses present an opportunity to acquaint prospective teachers with reflective study where design is a subject of investigation rather than a process for making something. However, most art history or arts studies classes rarely include a discussion of design in the syllabus. In the rare instances where design is a subject of investigation in these classes, it is usually viewed as a subspecialty of art and described in aesthetic terms, apart from issues of use, social context, and process. College and university art and design programs must encourage enrollment of non-majors in general courses and develop substantive discussions of critical issues in design so that teachers can be better prepared to involve students in the reflective study of design and to include them in evaluating and discussing design's impact on the quality of life.

The job of preparing teachers in design-based learning strategies, however, cannot be left to schools of design. Most are underfunded and struggling to maintain their traditional studio teaching practices in academic environments increasingly influenced by the efficiency standards that argue in favor of large lecture classes. They are unlikely to expand their missions significantly without additional resources. Furthermore, schools of design are not always in proximity to the strongest education programs. While there are as many as 500 four-year art and design programs that teach at least some courses in graphic design, many of the most effective are in private art colleges where there are no teacher education programs. Architecture programs exist in 100 institutions, and industrial design is an even smaller discipline of study with fewer than 50 programs. Collaborations between schools of education and schools of design—and broader access to design courses for education majors—is a fundamentally sound strategy that should be encouraged, but the small numbers of design faculty argue against this approach as a means for expanding design-based practices in U.S. schools.

The most promising approach is to introduce design-based instruction into schools of education. By training education professors in the content and methods of design, or by hiring designers as part of their teaching staffs, college and university education programs can support the development of well-informed teaching professionals who use design-based methods in their schools.

The most obvious place for such integration is in teaching methods courses. The first university design and education Master's degree program began in 1995 at California State Polytechnic University at Pomona. Doreen Nelson, with a joint teaching appointment in the Colleges of Education and Environmental Design, launched a Master of Arts program in education, focusing on design and creativity. Smaller scale efforts include the work of Charles Burnette and Jan Norman at the University of the Arts in Philadelphia; Susan Dunn at Lewis and Clark College in Portland, Oregon; and Meredith Davis and Robin Moore at North Carolina State University in Raleigh. Clearly, others will emerge. To maximize and sustain impact, however, it is important that these programs not become islands of specialization within an otherwise unchanged system of teacher preparation. The achievements of teachers who use design-based pedagogy show promise that other teachers' work can be enhanced by design education.

By hiring designers as part of their teaching staffs, education programs can support the development of well-informed teaching professionals who use design-based methods in their schools.

Supporting Systemwide Change

THIS BOOK POINTS out the importance of systemwide support for the work of design-based teachers and learners. Across the history of the design in education movement, we find many examples of successful teachers abandoning design-based strategies because the energy required to sustain innovative teaching in the face of administrative indifference was too great. In many cases, these teachers also lacked teaching peers who shared their interest in design; they had no counsel for their own teaching problems and no follow-up support for their students. Just as important, their school systems lacked reference materials and substantive research to support the decision to pursue a design approach to teaching.

As reported throughout this study, teachers who have administrative support for the use of design in classrooms achieve rich outcomes with their students and sustain success across the school

Administrative support includes knowledgeable principals and curriculum specialists who understand the fundamental processes of design.

year and from one year's class to the next. Such schools support an atmosphere of innovation and the creative involvement of teachers in curriculum development. These educators also are effective members of teaching teams because their school ensures conditions that foster joint planning, instruction, and assessment. Student achievements build progressively from one class to the next and from year to year because the school consistently places high value on thinking and open-ended inquiry, rather than on the acquisition of facts and mastery of skills detached from holistic problem solving.

Administrative support includes knowledgeable principals and curriculum specialists who understand the fundamental processes of design inquiry and the impact of design-based teaching and learning. They are able to make changes in the structure of the school day, allocate resources, and hire teacher colleagues who facilitate the use of design in the classroom. They share responsibility for, rather than dictate, curriculum, and they include a broad set of performances in their definitions of teacher assessment. In student assessment, they show more interest in substantive learning results than in reporting; they see assessment as ongoing feedback about student learning accomplishments that helps teachers

confirm or redirect strategies. They are slow to make judgments on the basis of a single activity and support innovation in the interest of long-term achievement.

Through well-communicated presentations of philosophy and goals, these strong administrators use their positions to attract community professionals and parents into the classroom. They involve themselves in the active life of the school and make frequent visits to classrooms and student presentations. Evidence of student work fills the physical environment of their schools, and they tolerate rearrangement of rooms and furniture. They provide a well-articulated vision of teaching and learning that inspires teachers and sustains focused commitment across time.

To become such an administrator requires experience and education. To date, most design-based training programs are for classroom teachers; curriculum specialists occasionally participate. While principals often endorse teacher participation in design education programs, they themselves rarely attend lectures and workshops as students of this approach. Furthermore, existing workshops fail to address the pressing concerns of principals and other school, district, and state administrators: raising test scores, the success rate of graduates, keeping children in school, and working with decreasing

Substantiating Achievement Through Credible Assessment

budgets. Workshops that show administrators how design-based programs contribute to meeting school-level challenges are necessary to expand the influence of these practices in schools. Research that analyzes and documents successful implementation of design-based approaches in other schools is needed to convince and support administrators who decide to pursue alternative strategies.

Just as design-based teaching depends on supportive administration in schools, principals of schools that use design look for confirmation that districts and states value their schools' teaching and learning achievements. District and state departments of public instruction should lead and foster educational reform to prevent single schools from becoming refreshing oases in an otherwise mediocre educational environment. To accomplish this, state administrators should fund and pilot studies and publish research in the use of design-based strategies. They should promote the successes of design-based learning and provide training for schools that wish to learn about its methods and outcomes. Because of the movement to site-based management of schools, administrators also should educate the public about design approaches to learning before wider adoption can take place.

THE ANECDOTAL information provided by the committed, professional educators contacted for this study, as well as the on-site observations and numerous interviews conducted by the research team, reveal compelling evidence of the benefits of design-based teaching and learning. Furthermore, there are strong correlations between design education methods and many of the curricular objectives and instructional approaches being advocated by leading researchers and education reformers today.

Nevertheless, before schools, districts, states, and teacher education programs embrace the use of design in the classroom, they must be convinced of its success. This study only opens the door onto a subject with a myriad of educational dimensions to explore. To broaden the influence of design in education in the United States and extend its benefits to more of the nation's students, educators must go beyond telling stories to develop appropriate, authentic instruments for determining student and program success.

Developing and maintaining the administration of performance-based tests, in which the form of the test demands application of the skills and content being tested, will not be easy. Myron Atkin at Stanford University notes: "There is a lot of nostalgia

about assessment. People support tests that look like tests used to look. California has experimented with performance-based assessment, but it is very expensive and people are impatient. They turn to something else when results are not immediate. What we're looking at in education today won't be there six or seven years from now; the political cycles exert pressure to deliver quick results. Politicians believe they have a strong role to play in what educators do. This is not true in Europe, where the teaching profession is more highly respected, so you will see much greater strides in reform and assessment in other countries."

Kathryn Loncar, Associate Professor of Education at the University of Missouri, conducted a review of Ginny Graves' design-based curriculum, *Walk Around the Block.* Her study confirms that rigorous assessment is one challenge facing proponents. She says, "To be convincing and to promote design in education, we need documentation of student performance on standardized tests." She feels the anecdotal evidence is persuasive, but in the current political climate, numbers count.

Susan Dunn, former instructional coordinator at Willamette Primary School, says her current school gives standardized tests, but fewer than before the adoption of design-based

In research terms, the major dependent variables of schooling are not scores on standardized tests, whether norm- or criterion-referenced: they are the kinds of ideas children are willing to explore on their own, the kinds of critical skills they are able to employ on tasks outside classrooms, and the strength of their curiosity in pursuing the issues they will inevitably encounter in the course of their lives.

ELLIOT EISNER, *What Really Counts in Schools*

sharing with others what you have done

approaches. They are used more as an audit of how well everyone is doing. She believes, however, that assessment is "sharing with others what you have done, which includes people who hold evaluation responsibility," such as principals and instructional coordinators. Dunn says, "This evaluation can't be punitive and must encourage risk taking. Furthermore, administrators need to be teaching in the classroom to assess this approach." Dunn also encourages her teachers to talk about learning in their classrooms with the phrase "When our students are doing design…" rather than saying, "Our children do design." This forces teachers to complete the phrase with a description of learning outcomes that gives outsiders a better picture of student achievement and frames their accomplishments in terms of thinking skills, rather than cute products.

Educational psychologist Leona Schauble comments that, "Design externalizes evidence of how students think and lets how they think govern teaching. The evaluation criteria are public in the classroom, unlike other forms of assessment."

As demonstrated by the schools in this study, performance-based and portfolio assessment seem appropriate methods for measuring individual student learning. These methods are consistent with the latest research in learning and assessment, and they provide useful feedback to teachers, students, and parents. They also employ dimensions critical to the design process, including:

- evaluation of holistic problem solving in which thinking and doing are as important as the products of thought and action;

- assessment across time, rather than as single measurement at one moment in time; and

- accommodation of differences in students' learning preferences and ways of demonstrating mastery.

Yet there is little agreement within and among these schools, even in similar subject areas and grade levels, about what constitutes an appropriate portfolio of work, the criteria against which teachers and schools measure

excellence, and the ways in which teachers and schools report individual learning achievements. While many of the teachers in our study are clear about assessment criteria and strategies for individual projects, they offer little insight as to how the projects fit into the overall assessment of student performance in their subject area or among subjects where cross-disciplinary strategies occur.

Further, design-based educators have yet to develop effective ways for linking individual student assessments to the evaluation of schools and districts. While the work in the United Kingdom offers insight into large-scale assessment, the British adoption of a national curriculum has no parallel in U.S. education. Despite promotion of voluntary national standards in core subjects, movement toward site-based management and local curriculum control present even greater challenges to reporting statistically significant outcomes from the use of design in U.S. classrooms.

Because design is frequently the method of inquiry, rather than the subject of inquiry, it is often difficult to attribute learning achievements to the presence of design in the curriculum through periodic assessment in core subjects. The New Standards project (described in Appendix A) shows

Teacher Resources

promise in capturing this type of learning success through its assessment of Applied Learning. In these performance-based exercises, students test a range of problem-solving skills that are not linked to specific school subjects and that share much in common with the design activities described earlier in this report.

Clearly, the task ahead is to develop and implement assessment criteria and strategies that will produce reliable and valid evidence of design-based education's value, in terms understandable to parents as well as educators. This must be done within the current context of "reporting and accountability" that characterizes U.S. education, while remaining true to the nature of design activity and learning. At the same time, the advocates and practitioners of design-based education should demonstrate the common elements among national voluntary standards in core subjects—problem-solving mastery, communication skills, critical thinking, linking school with life and work—and connect their achievement to design-based teaching strategies and curricula through credible assessment.

THOSE WHO TRAIN teachers in design-based methods report frequent requests for reference materials on design and teaching design to help educators continue their study after workshops end. Other teachers comment that wider availability of design-based lesson plans in various disciplines would provide useful models from which they could build their own projects.

Plainly, there are few resources through which teachers and administrators can learn about design and the use of design in education. The publications that do exist are hard to find and not widely publicized in teacher journals. While experts debate the advisability of developing prepackaged programs that do not take into account the characteristics of individual schools and classrooms, it is clear that literature to support instruction is needed if college and university teacher education programs are to invest in design-based curriculum development.

While some publishers include more project suggestions in the teacher's editions of their books in response to increased interest in active learning, most write textbooks as if they were lectures. Even many interactive media products organize content in structures that resemble passive books, not interactive hypertext environments. These products often ignore divergent learn-

ing strategies that allow students to move through content in a self-determined order according to their specific needs. Rarely are interactive media programs linked to physical activity outside the computer or to solving a problem for which the programmer has no predictable solution. The next move for authors of design-based curricula should be to collaborate with textbook publishers and developers of curriculum materials. Once textbooks reflect these innovative strategies, there will be wider use of design methods.

Among the resources teachers need is a network of other teachers using design in the classroom. Curriculum control necessarily resides at state and local levels in the United States, yet

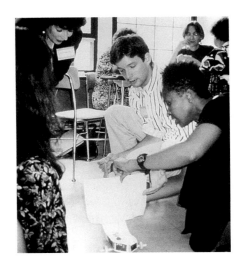

Participants in a Cooper-Hewitt National Design Museum workshop test their creation.

elementary and secondary teachers anywhere in the country have a wealth of support systems to rely upon and can benefit from the insights and innovations of their peers in areas such as curriculum development, instructional practice, and assessment techniques. Among these support systems are state and district specialists in various disciplines, state and national associations linking members by grade level or subject area, technical assistance hotlines, Web sites, and workshops offered by textbook and software publishers, and newsletters distributed by various education reform initiatives.

In contrast, teachers attempting to integrate design topics and methods into their practice are relatively isolated from one another and from researchers, curriculum developers, and other advocates of design-based learning. At present, no organization coordinates a national network of teachers, workshops, or the distribution of materials related to the use of design in K-12 classrooms. Nor have special interest groups focusing on design methods emerged within the major discipline-based teacher associations.

Instead there are numerous complementary, but generally unconnected, efforts relating to design-based education. As recounted earlier in this book, some are based in community institutions such as museums or local chapters of professional design associations; others are tied to schools of education, schools of design, or nonprofit organizations with a regional or national scope. Still others are short-lived, multiyear projects funded by federal agencies or foundations. In each case, the individuals involved may develop and even publish curriculum materials relating to design in education. But often these materials are printed in limited editions or receive insufficient marketing to attract a national audience.

The institutions that house pioneering design education programs also may present unintended impediments to the broad dissemination of their work. Some authors of relevant curricula are designers who teach part-time in schools of education, or they may be the only faculty with K-12 interests in schools of design. Professional design associations, while supportive of K-12 initiatives, have other concerns that frequently take budget and program precedence over primary and secondary education. Furthermore, these associations generally focus on one design discipline, and their school programs follow suit.

Public and private sector funders of pilot projects, curriculum development,

A teacher, ideally conceived, is a designer who helps learners to design themselves.

DAVID PERKINS, *Knowledge as Design*, p. 230

or other research directly focused on design in education may also be unaware of their overlapping interests and not informed of the progress made by each other's grantees. At the federal level alone, the Department of Education, Department of Energy, Environmental Protection Agency, National Endowment for the Arts, National Endowment for the Humanities, National Science Foundation, and other agencies have all funded projects relevant to design in education (whether or not their design dimensions were fully articulated and explored). Similarly, relevant projects receive funding from numerous private and corporate foundations, sometimes under the aegis of science and math reform, at other times in the areas of art education, technology, and school-business partnerships. With rare exceptions, however, few of these funders work jointly across disciplines. Neither do they support pilot projects or research efforts with adequate resources or over sufficient periods of time to enable painstaking assessment of learning outcomes, longitudinal study of student populations, or widespread dissemination of results.

As this book shows, however, teachers who see the relevance of design to their practice and its multiple benefits to their students' lives and learning can be found in all corners of the United States, teaching all grade levels and subject areas, working both alone and with other teachers, and reaching all types of students. Surely there is a critical mass of developing interest, which—if supported by strategic investments in networking, preservice training, resource dissemination, and further research—will lead to a quantum leap in the integration of design methods across the spectrum of U.S. education. Design will then have a positive, catalytic influence not only on students' learning, but also on U.S. schools and communities.

Reference

The Holmes Group. (1995). *Tomorrow's Schools of Education.* East Lansing, Michigan: The Holmes Group, Inc.

---

1 In 1996, The Holmes Group became The Holmes Partnership, 101 Willard Hall Education Building, University of Delaware, Newark, Delaware 19716.

DESIGN EDUCATION
in the Context of Education Reform

t he relevance of a design approach to teaching and learning is evident when viewed within the context of education reform. After more than a decade of heralding the need to improve schools, educators still search for practical strategies for achieving reform goals. This summary of recent reform initiatives illustrates the connections between our national aspirations for improving education and the outcomes of incorporating design experiences in K-12 classrooms.

A Nation at Risk

THE 1983 REPORT of the National Commission on Excellence in Education expressed what many educators and policymakers long believed: Deteriorating academic performance would soon lead to significant social and economic problems in the United States. The report was blunt about the implications for the country. "Our once unchallenged preeminence in commerce, industry, science and technological innovation is being overtaken by competitors throughout the world." This powerful report focused national attention on the fact that our schools were no longer adequate to prepare students for successful adult lives.

Despite considerable debate over the possible reasons for the decline in U.S. education—including insufficient funding for schools, decline in standards of excellence, increase in the number of students placed at risk, loss of common values, poor teacher training, inadequate leadership, irrelevant curricula, and lack of community support—several

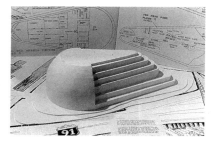

areas of consensus have emerged over the past decade. Parents, teachers, administrators, and community leaders in the debate tend to agree that:

- Many schools do not develop in children the basic skills, knowledge, and attitudes necessary to become productive adults.

- All schools must build connections among the academic disciplines and between in-school experiences and the rest of children's lives.

- A successful life in the 21st century will depend less on mastery of specific facts and more on skill in accessing, analyzing, organizing, and acting upon information. There is an increasing need to use knowledge, rather than simply acquire it.

- All schools must engage students in ways that respond to their natural curiosity and individual ways of learning, providing multiple points of entry into subject matter and a variety of assessment strategies.

Attempts to achieve these reform goals began in the United States in the 1980s. Initial efforts tightened, and in the case of the arts increased, high school graduation requirements and increased periodic standardized testing of students at all levels. Later came the decentralization of program management in many school systems, providing principals, teachers, and parents a greater say in what is taught, by whom, and how. Experiments in site-based management empowered teachers to make local decisions about curriculum, assessment, and educational policy. A few districts have extended the school day or lengthened the school calendar in the belief that time in the classroom contributed to the quality of student performance. More recently, even greater numbers of districts have instituted "block schedules," lengthening the time spent on a subject in a single period in high school, but requiring only a total of four subjects per day.

However, in spite of these and other developments since 1983, as Diane Massell and colleagues (Massell, Fuhrman, Kirst, Odden, Wohlstetter, Carver, and Yee 1993, p. 5) observe in their review of education reform over the last decade, "The kind of standard-setting launched by *A Nation at Risk* did not directly address the academic content of schooling. It required more seat time in courses labeled science and mathematics, for example, but did not insure the quality of science and mathematics courses that students would receive."

As reform efforts have continued, educators have placed increasing attention on the nature and content of instruction. In 1988, the National Council of Teachers of Mathematics (NCTM) issued a set of grade-specific standards for mathematics. These standards remain the model for defining national content objectives in other disciplines.

A watershed event in efforts to establish national priorities for education improvement was the 1987 publication of *Workforce 2000: Work and Workers for the 21st Century.* This report established a national framework for what students must achieve, and it deliberately linked the nation's future economic prosperity to the quality of today's education. In response to this overarching summary of the nation's need for a well-educated and occupationally flexible workforce,

Goals 2000

a number of public and private-sponsored commissions and task forces went to work devising strategies to meet the challenges posed in this seminal report. Three have direct relevance to design-based learning. They are: Goals 2000 and the formalization of national education policy, The Secretary's Commission on Achieving Necessary Skills (SCANS), and voluntary national content standards in basic subjects, including the arts.

More recently, the work of the New Standards Project, a collaboration of the Learning Research and Development Center (LRDC) at the University of Pittsburgh and the National Center on Education and the Economy (NCEE), holds promise for building an assessment system that measures student progress in meeting national standards. The assessment system has three components: performance descriptions in English/language arts, mathematics, science, and applied learning; an on-demand examination; and a portfolio assessment system. Of particular relevance to the discussion of design approaches to teaching and learning are the performance descriptions in applied learning and the portfolio assessment.

FROM A HISTORIC summit in 1989, jointly convened by the National Governors Association and President George Bush, came national goals for education that, with some revisions, Congress codified as Federal policy in 1994 in the Goals 2000: Educate America Act. These eight goals describe the conditions and outcomes for education and list core subjects in which all students must achieve mastery of skills and knowledge. The Goals 2000 legislation added two goals to the original six developed in 1989 and includes the arts among the core subjects outlined in Goal 3. The use of design in education holds great significance for achieving several of these goals.

The full language of Goal 3 expresses concern for students' thinking and problem-solving skills by indicating that "all students learn to use their minds well." The implication is that schools currently pay less attention to building students' full range of cognitive abilities than to the subjects of their thought. Design-based learning, on the other hand, places a high value on examining modes of inquiry and developing flexible thinking skills that are useful across disciplines. Furthermore, more children succeed in classrooms when the instructional approaches tolerate and encourage a variety of learning styles and modes of inquiry.

Goal 4 calls for excellent preservice and inservice training of teachers. While most college programs prepare teachers in the subjects they will later teach, college curricula lag behind in developing and disseminating new teaching methods that respond to the most recent research about how children learn. Many teacher education programs fail to equip teachers with the thinking skills necessary to invent new learning experiences or a vision of themselves as more than the repositories of data.

As this book illustrates, there is impressive evidence that teachers who use design in their classrooms are more excited about teaching and view themselves as creative professionals. There is also confirmation that these teachers acquire their skill with innovation through sources other than their college or university education and that they are ambassadors for a design approach with their teaching colleagues. Because design-based approaches to teaching transcend the boundaries of subject matter, address the diversity of student learning styles, and actively engage teachers in building innovative curricula, design education shows great promise as a model for reforming teacher education.

Goal 6 emphasizes the creation of a literate and productive workforce, prepared for competition in the global economy and active in the life of the

Goal 1: All children in America will start school ready to learn.

Goal 2: The high school graduation rate will increase to at least 90%.

Goal 3: All students will leave grades 4, 8, and 12 having demonstrated competency over challenging subject matter including English, mathematics, science, foreign languages, civics and government, economics, the arts, history, and geography.

Goal 4: U.S. students will be first in the world in mathematics and science achievement.

Goal 5: Every adult American will be literate and will possess the knowledge and skills necessary to compete in a global economy and exercise the rights and responsibilities of citizenship.

Goal 6: Every school in the United States will be free of drugs, violence, and the unauthorized presence of firearms and alcohol, and will offer a disciplined environment conducive to learning.

Goal 7: The nation's teaching force will have access to programs for the continued improvement of their professional skills.

Goal 8: Every school will promote partnerships that will increase parental involvement and participation in promoting the social, emotional, and academic growth of children.

Design activities teach
children to make intelligent
choices about technology, to
design technology to
solve problems,
and to **define** the preferred
role of machines
in their lives.

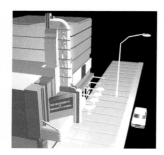

community. The use of design in the classroom achieves these objectives. Ours is an increasingly visual world; literate adults are those who can interpret, judge, and act upon visual as well as verbal and quantitative information. Television, magazines, and newspapers like *USA Today* demand discriminating readers of visual messages. Design activities teach students to communicate fluently in both visual and verbal modes of expression and to be critical readers of information in all forms. Design experiences frequently employ modeling and diagramming that reveal the true nature of information and the complex relationships among ideas. If students are to be masters of information and not unknowing victims of persuasion, they must develop visual literacy at levels equal to their command of verbal language.

Technological literacy will be equally important in the next century. Citizens without access to information networks risk exclusion from democratic processes and decision making in their work and communities. A technologically unskilled workforce faces extinction. Yet

simply acquiring software skills is not sufficient to address the goal of technological literacy. Literacy also is about knowing what to say and how to say it. Students must know when to use specific technologies and how to account for the degree to which tools determine outcomes. They need to be critical users of technology who demand human-centered, rather than machine-centered, approaches to solving problems.

Design experiences integrate technology instruction with the goal of solving human dilemmas. Designers think of technology as "a choice about the way to do things," rather than as a predetermined method of operation or a tool. Their models can be sophisticated three-dimensional computer diagrams or wooden sticks held together with glue. Each informs its creator and others in different ways. Design activities teach children to make intelligent choices about technology, to design technology to solve problems, and to define the preferred role of machines in their lives.

Exercising the rights and responsibilities of citizenship demands a range of skills not often fostered by traditional teaching practices. Schools usually encourage individual performance at the expense of shared accomplishment. Where team assignments exist, they frequently lack an explicit framework for working together and leave stu-

dents skeptical about relinquishing control of tasks to their peers. Design activities, on the other hand, involve students in the process of choice, usually as members of teams focused on solving a single problem. The design process guides their work, introducing structured critique and collective judgment throughout the process. Through such experiences, children learn teamwork and strategies for participation in issues and labor that involve differing points of view. The design process provides a clear structure for generating alternatives, making choices, and resolving conflicts of opinion.

Design activities also challenge students to explore the social and cultural contexts implicit in their design tasks. The subjects of their investigation are often the very issues they will confront as adults: the location of a city park, the match between the architecture of a public building and the values of a community, solutions to community recycling of discarded products, and visual communications that encourage and inform public debate on important issues. Design experiences, unlike those in many other academic disciplines, require no special translation to life outside of school. They engage students in content and model practical processes that are intrinsic to life as responsible citizens.

The Secretary's Commission on Achieving Necessary Skills (SCANS)

THE U.S. DEPARTMENT of Labor convened representatives from education, business, labor, and government to identify the skills and competencies that workers of the future will need "to encourage a high performance economy characterized by high-skills, high-wage employment." The final report, issued in July 1992, named five competencies and a three-part foundation of skills and personal qualities the Commission believed necessary for strong future job performance (see Figure A-1).

The SCANS recommendations provide curricular and pedagogical frameworks for preparing students for adult life and pose a substantial challenge to the major institutions charged with responsibility for developing worker competencies. The report distinguishes, in a commonsense way, the elements of being "educated" and then introduces a set of higher-order competencies necessary for successful participation in future economics and politics.

Of particular relevance to the use of design in schools are the five competencies identified by the National Board on Workplace Skills as central to the productive workforce of the future:

− use and manipulation of information,

− use and allocation of available resources,

− use of technology,

− understanding and use of systems, and

− use of interpersonal skills.

Figure A.1

Key Worker Competencies, Skills, and Qualities Identified by Scans				
Competencies for Productive Work		**The Foundation for Effective Mastery and Use of Key Competencies**		
Use of Resources	Allocates time, money, materials, space, and staff to achieve desired ends	**Basic Skills**	**Thinking Skills**	**Personal Qualities**
Use of Information	Acquires and evaluates information; Organizes and maintains information; Interprets and communicates information; Uses computers to process information	Reading	Creative thinking	Responsibility
		Writing	Decision-making	Self-esteem
Interpersonal Skills	Participates as a member of a team; Teaches others; Serves clients/customers; Exercises leadership; Negotiates to arrive at a decision; Works with people with culturally diverse backgrounds	Arithmetic	Problem-solving	Sociability
		Mathematics	Seeing things in the mind's eye	Self-management
Using Systems	Understands systems; Monitors and corrects performance; Improves and designs systems	Listening	Knowing how to learn	Integrity/honesty
Using Technology	Selects technology; Applies technology to task; Maintains and trobleshoots technology	Speaking	Reasoning	

Source: The Secretary's Commission on Achieving Necessary Skills, *What Work Requires of Schools: A SCANS Report for America 2000* (Washington D.C.: U.S. Department of Labor).

Many of the reasons for using design activities to achieve SCANS objectives are the same as those discussed with reference to Goals 2000, yet a few require elaboration in terms of how design relates to the SCANS report.

While a literate citizenry knows how to interpret, judge, and act on information, its members also must be active makers of messages and able to manipulate information in ways that lead to the discovery or application of new knowledge. Design activities develop the ability to enhance and transform ideas through the visualization, manipulation, and application of data to problem solving. Through design projects, students learn to reveal meaning in facts, to view the same information from many viewpoints, and to expose various dimensions of data through alternate forms of presentation.

While the role technology plays in this manipulation and application of data is increasingly important to work, so is the development of technology itself. Design projects encourage the invention of new ways of doing work more efficiently. Beginning with simple projects and moving to complex technological solutions, design-based education encourages students not to accept the limitations of current technology in the solution of problems. Instead, they should invent the means for doing something, as well as the solution itself.

Also among the strengths of design-based education is student learning about the use and allocation of resources. Through design projects, students gain firsthand experience in closing the distance between the resources they think are necessary for the very best solution to the problem and what they can afford. They learn to view objects and environments in terms of their total life cycle (from raw materials to disposal or reuse), increasing their awareness of the environmental, social, and economic consequences of design decisions. Students also learn to assess quality in terms of the integrity of materials and the processes that shape them. Finally, students learn about human resources and that the solution to a problem may not be physical but social. They discover the efficiency and effectiveness of teamwork and planning, as well as the economic value of processes such as prototyping and formative evaluation.

Voluntary National Content and Performance Standards

THE THIRD MAJOR initiative for U.S. national education reform in the early to mid-1990s was the development of a coordinated effort to articulate curricular expectations for core subjects in the schools. Following the announcement of national education goals by the governors and the White House in 1989, a working group of governors recommended voluntary national standards as a yardstick against which to measure achievement. In response, Congress established a special council to examine expert opinion regarding appropriate high-level standards of achievement in various disciplines. The intent was "to raise the ceiling for students who are currently above average and to lift the floor for those who now experience the least success in school, including those with special needs" (The National Council on Education Standards and Testing 1992).

The National Council of Teachers of Mathematics published its suggested standards for mathematics in 1988. Based in part on the conclusions and recommendations of the report of the National Council on Education Standards and Testing, the U.S. Department of Education solicited proposals and awarded grants for standard-setting projects in a number of core subjects. Voluntary national standards in the arts (dance, music, theatre, and the visual arts) were completed and disseminated in early 1994, followed by voluntary standards in U.S. and world history, geography, civics and government, science, and English/language arts.

The standards describe what every American student should know and be able to do in various disciplines, representing "a common vision of competence and educational effectiveness ... not how those results ought to be delivered" (Consortium of National Arts Education Associations 1994, p. 12). Through a consensus process, organizations charged with developing standards articulated content and achievement standards for students at grades 4, 8, and 12. While developers of the National Standards for Arts Education made efforts to include design, the work of other disciplines also reflects competencies that can be achieved through design-based strategies and teaching attitudes that are consistent with a design approach.

As the voluntary standards in the core subjects of the National Education Goals emerge, as well as the expectations they convey for what students should know and are able to do, they must inform the design and implementation of assessments. The means for gauging our progress as a nation toward achieving these high expectations in core subjects is through the National Assessment of Educational Progress (NAEP), which is funded by Congress and commonly referred to as The Nation's Report Card. NAEP periodically assesses students in grades 4, 8, and 12 in the core subject areas listed in the National Education Goals. The National Assessment of Educational Progress in the Arts, scheduled for 1997, is one of the first NAEP subject assessments to be based on the voluntary national standards and to use performance-based projects in visual art and design. The next comprehensive NAEP assessment in the arts is scheduled for 2007.

National reform efforts reflect government and industry concern that our schools view their decisions about instruction and curriculum within the context of the society in which students will perform as adults. They also acknowledge that emphasis must shift from acquiring discrete facts to learning processes that help people succeed within an environment characterized by a rapidly changing knowledge base. While the preceding initiatives focus on what children learn, others look for greater understanding of how they learn.

New Performance Standards in Applied Learning

"CONTENT STANDARDS specify 'what students should know and be able to do'; performance standards go the next step to specify 'how good is good enough'" (National Center on Education and the Economy [NCEE] and the University of Pittsburgh 1997, p. 3). Unlike discipline-specific standards, the performance standards in applied learning focus on "connecting the work students do in school with the demands of the twenty-first century workplace ... on the capabilities people need to be productive members of society, as individuals who apply the knowledge gained in school and elsewhere to analyze problems and propose solutions, to communicate effectively and coordinate action with others, and to use the tools of the information age in the workplace" (NCEE 1997, p. 5).

By drawing attention to distinct performance standards for applied learning, the authors establish a "domain for assessment and reporting student achievement" (NCEE 1997, p. 112). Assessing students' performance in applied learning is not an appeal for a new subject in American classrooms, but acknowledgment that such areas of competence apply to all subjects and within the context of cross-curricular learning experiences.

Problem solving is a primary concern of the standards. The performance description focuses on productive activity and three kinds of problem solving. Middle school students must conduct projects in at least two of the following:

- Design a product, service, or system in which the student identifies needs that could be met by new products, services, or systems and creates solutions for meeting them;

- Improve a system in which the student develops an understanding of the way systems of people, machines, and processes work; troubleshoots problems in their operation and devises strategies for improving their effectiveness;

- Plan and organize an event or activity in which the student takes responsibility for all aspects of planning and organizing an event or an activity from concept to completion (NCEE 1997, p. 112).

Standards related to "tools and techniques" center on the problem-solving standard and are "only meaningful when considered in the context of work that has a genuine purpose and audience" and "put to use in an integrated way" (NCEE 1997, p. 112). The standards calling for students to make effective use of information technology and to present project plans or results to audiences beyond the school overlap with other areas of competence. However, in all cases, evidence of achievement in these standards must be concrete and demonstrated through a work product.

References

Assessment activities aimed at evaluating student mastery of the performance standards bear striking resemblance to design projects mentioned earlier in this book. Designing and building a wheelchair access ramp, conducting an energy audit of the classroom and developing procedures for reducing waste, designing and conducting a community survey to inform local city or county council decisions about the future use of a community-owned building, and publishing a brochure advertising the school for new students are consistent with the activities developed by teachers identified through this study.

In the 1995-96 testing of applied learning portfolios, however, developers found most of the teachers and students in the 50 middle school test classrooms had no prior experience with such projects. Yet the development of assessment systems have a powerful effect on teaching practices and curricula in the United States. Assessments signal what society values in education and provide a means for describing the achievement of goals, effectiveness of practices, and relevance of outcomes. As future assessment strategies, whether at national, state, or local levels, value the knowledge and skills developed through design experiences, it is hoped that more teachers will apply design-based approaches in their classrooms.

Consortium of National Arts Education Associations. (1994). *National Standards for Arts Education.* Reston, Virginia: Music Educators National Conference.

Massell D., Fuhrman S., Kirst, M., Odden, A., Wohlstetter P., Carver, R., and Yee, G. (1993). *Ten Years of State Education Reform, 1983-1993.* New Brunswick, New Jersey: Consortium for Policy Research in Education.

National Assessment Governing Board. (1994). *NAEP Arts Education Consensus Project, Arts Education Assessment Framework* (Pre-publication edition). Washington, D.C.: The Chief State School Officers with the College Board and the Council for Basic Education.

National Center on Education and the Economy and the University of Pittsburgh. (1997). *Performance Standards, Volume 2, Middle School.* Washington, D.C.: National Center on Education and the Economy.

National Commission on Excellence in Education. (1983). *A Nation at Risk: The Imperative for Educational Reform.* Washington, D.C.: National Commission on Excellence in Education.

The National Council on Education Standards and Testing. (1992). *Raising Standards for American Education.* Washington, D.C.: Superintendent of Documents and Government Printing Office.

National Council of Teachers of Mathematics. (1989). *Curriculum and Evaluation Standards for School Mathematics.* Washington, D.C.: Working Groups of the Commission on Standards for School Mathematics of the National Council of Teachers of Mathematics.

National Endowment for the Arts. (1994). *Goals 2000: Opportunities for the Arts.* Washington, D.C.: National Endowment for the Arts, U.S. Department of Education, and National Assembly of State Arts Agencies.

The Secretary's Commission on Achieving Necessary Skills. (1991). *What Work Requires of Schools: A SCANS Report for America 2000.* Washington, D.C.: U.S. Department of Labor.

United States Department of Labor. (1992). *Skills and Tasks for Jobs, A SCANS Report for America 2000.* Washington, D.C.: United States Department of Labor.

United States Department of Labor, Employment and Training Administration. (1987). *Workforce 2000: Work and Workers for the 21st Century.* Washington, D.C.: prepared by the Hudson Institute for the Department of Labor, Superintendent of Documents.

SOURCES OF
Information and Assistance

there is no single source in the United States for information or assistance on the uses of design in elementary and secondary education. Just as many different elements—products, graphic communications, buildings, landscapes, and urban planning—go together to create the designed environment, so too do many different individuals and institutions constitute the web of allies upon which educators can draw.

At the most personal level, teachers in communities large and small usually can find design professionals who studied one or another of the disciplines mentioned above. Graphic designers, for example, may work for advertising agencies, publishers, corporate and university communications departments,

or in their own design firms. Planners, architects, and landscape architects may work for city and county governments, real estate development companies, conservation organizations, or in their own firms. Many design professionals are eager to help young people explore the many dimensions of design all around them and experience the excitement of creating new forms. While such professionals may be able to assist in integrating design topics and activities into the curriculum, they may also need some instruction themselves about the teacher's content and assessment objectives and about the abilities of children at various stages of cognitive and social development.

Beyond the level of individuals, many communities in the United

States have nonprofit organizations and institutions with expertise in design and an educational mission that includes working with elementary and secondary schools. Among these may be local or state chapters of professional design associations, schools of design, museums, and various nonprofit organizations dedicated to raising awareness about cultural heritage or environmental design quality.

In many cities and counties there may be a historic preservation organization with education staff or trained volunteers who can help students explore the evolution of their own community, its buildings, and surrounding landscape. While some programs focus specifically on understanding how construction techniques and architectural styles changed over time, others engage young people in the examination of contemporary planning, design, and preservation issues in both town and countryside. Similarly, local environmental groups and nature centers may be sources of information and activities enabling students to explore the many connections between natural resource issues and the design of products and places.

Serving larger cities and metropolitan regions there may be additional institutions with information and educational expertise in one or more aspects of design. Many children's museums and science and technology centers, for example, have interactive exhibits on such subjects as architecture and engineering, product design, and graphic design in print and electronic forms. Art museums and history museums may have collections encompassing one or more of the design disciplines. In addition to their on-site resources, many of these institutions may have outreach programs specifically tailored to K-12 schools, including inservice workshops for teachers, curriculum units for classroom use, and periodic in-school learning activities. At a minimum, the education staff at such museums are good sources of information about other organizations that can assist teachers interested in developing more expertise in using design.

At the national level, there are a few non-profit institutions and organizations specifically devoted to advancing the use of design in elementary and secondary schools. Many of these have newsletters, publish or distribute curriculum materials, and conduct teacher education. Other organizations may focus primarily on reaching and educating leaders in business and government about the importance of design to the nation's economy and the quality of life in its communities. These groups also may have materials that teachers can use with secondary school students or adapt for younger grades.

Each of the design disciplines has one or more national organizations. At a minimum they distribute general information about their field, career opportunities, and accredited colleges and universities. Many have publication catalogs or bookstores that carry print and audio-visual materials on design topics for a general audience, as well as more technical materials for design professionals. Increasingly, national design organizations reach out to young people in both formal and informal educational settings. Some include print and audio-visual materials specifically for children in their catalogs. A few have taken the next step by carrying curriculum materials for K-12 teachers or by working

with educators to develop new materials for classroom use.

While national design organizations may encourage their state and local affiliates to work with elementary and secondary schools, such programs are usually at the discretion of individual chapters or members. State and local chapters, or components, of the American Institute of Architects have been particularly active in establishing on-going programs to assist teachers in many parts of the country. Often these are administered by a separate non-profit organization or "foundation" established by the chapter to carry out public awareness-raising activities and more formal educational programs.

In addition to institutions with expertise in one or more of the design fields, organizations dedicated to design in K-12 education, and the design professions themselves, there are a myriad of professional education groups whose interests overlap design to one degree or another. As this book has shown, teachers in every academic area and at every grade level have found that the use of design benefits their practice and their students' learning. While few education organizations have specific programs devoted to design, they may have staff expertise, materials, and inservice opportunities in one or more related areas, such as project-based learning, performance assessment, or school-to-work transition, that teachers using design within a single discipline or in an interdisciplinary program might find useful.

The following list, while selective, attempts to encompass the wide range of organizations to which teachers can turn for information, assistance, or simply just for communication with their colleagues about various aspects of design in K-12 education. As that dialogue increases across discipline boundaries, grade levels, and even international borders, it will undoubtedly stimulate new approaches to the use of design across the curriculum, innovative collaborations, and ultimately excellent practice in America's classrooms.

Sources in the United States

American Center for Design
325 W. Huron Street, Suite 711
Chicago, IL 60610
312-787-2018
fax: 312-649-9518
e-mail: acd@aol.com
http://www.ac4d.org

American Association for the
Advancement of Science, Project 2061
1333 H Street, NW
Washington, DC 20005
202-326-6666
http://www.aaas.org

American Institute of Architects
and American Architectural Foundation
(Learning by Design Program)
1735 New York Avenue, NW
Washington, DC 20006
202-626-7300
http://www.aiaonline.com

American Institute of Graphic Arts
164 Fifth Avenue
New York, NY 10010
212-807-1990
fax: 212-807-1799
e-mail: AIGAnswers@aiga.org
http://www.aiga.org

American Planning Association
122 S. Michigan Avenue, Suite 1600
Chicago, IL 60603
312-431-9100
fax: 312-431-9985

American Society of Interior Designers
608 Massachusetts Avenue, NE
Washington, DC 20002-6006
202-546-3480
http://www.asid.org

American Society of Landscape Architects
636 Eye Street, NW
Washington, DC 20001
202-898-2444
http://www.asla.org

ArtsEdge
A National Arts Education
Information Network
202-416-8871
http://artsedge.kennedy-center.org/

Association of Science
and Technology Centers
1025 Vermont Avenue, NW, Suite 500
Washington, DC 20005
202-783-7200
http://www.astc.org/astc

Association for Supervision and
Curriculum Development
1250 North Pitt Street
Alexandria, VA 22314-1453
703-549-9110 or 1-800-933-2723
http://www.ascd.org

Building Connections
730 E. Three Fountains Drive #84
Murray, UT 84107-5250
801-262-4449

Building Environmental
Education Solutions, Inc.
685 College Road East
Princeton, NJ 08543-7201
609-243-4507
fax: 609-951-8410
http://www.bees.org

Center for City Building Education
2118 Wilshire Boulevard #303
Santa Monica, CA 90403
310-471-0090
fax: 310-471-1955
e-mail: doreennelson@earthlink.net
http://www.citybuilding.edu

Center for Civic Education
5146 Douglas Fir Road
Calabasas, CA 91302-1467
818-591-9321
fax: 818-591-9330
http://www.primenet.com/~cce

Center for Understanding
the Built Environment
5328 W. 67th Street
Prairie Village, KS 66208
913-262-0691
fax: 913-262-8546
e-mail: ginny@cubekc.org
http://www.cubekc.org

Chicago Architecture Foundation
224 S. Michigan Avenue
Chicago, IL 60604-2507
312-922-3432
fax: 312-922-0481
http://www.architecture.org

Connecticut Architecture Foundation,
Architecture Resource Center
87 Willow Street
New Haven, CT 06511
203-865-2195
fax: 203-562-5378

Cooper-Hewitt, National Design
Museum, Smithsonian Institution
2 E. 91st Street
New York, NY 10128
Education Department:
212-860-6868
fax: 212-860-6909
http://www.si.edu/ndm

Corporate Design Foundation
CHECK
20 Park Plaza, Suite 321
Boston, MA 02116
617-350-7097
fax: 617-451-6355
e-mail: admin@cdf.org
http://www.cdf.org

Design Based Education K-12
University of the Arts
Art Education Department
320 S. Broad Street,
Philadelphia, PA 19102
215-875-4881
fax: 215-875-5467
http://www.uarts.edu/~arts

Design Management Institute
29 Temple Place
Boston, MA 02111-1350
617-338-6380
fax: 617-338-6570
e-mail: dmistaff@dmi.org
http://www.dmi.org

Getty Education Institute for the Arts
1200 Getty Center Drive, Suite 600
Los Angeles, CA 90049-1683
310-440-7315
fax: 310-440-7704
http://www.artsednet.getty.edu/

Goals 2000 Arts Education Partnership
One Massachusetts Avenue, NW, Suite 700
Washington, DC 20001-1431

Foundation for Architecture, Architecture
in Education Program
1617 JFK Boulevard, Suite 1165
Philadelphia, PA 19103
215-569-3187
fax: 215-569-4688
e-mail: aie@whyy.org
http://www.whyy.org/aie

The Holmes Partnership
101 Willard Hall, Education Building
University of Delaware
Newark, DE 19716
302-831-2557
fax: 302-831-3013
http://www.udel.edu/holmes/

Industrial Designers Society of America
1142 Walker Road, Suite E
Great Falls, VA 22066
703-759-0100
fax: 703-759-7679
e-mail: idsa@erols.com
http://www.idsa.org

Institute for Research on Learning
66 Willow Place
Menlo Park, CA 94025-3601
415-614-7900
fax: 415-614-7957
http://www.irl.org

International Technology Education
Association
1914 Association Drive
Reston, VA 20191-1539
703-860-2100
fax: 703-860-0353
e-mail: itea@iris.org
http://www.iteawww.org

Kennedy Center Alliance for Art
Education Network
John F. Kennedy Center
Education Department
Washington, DC 20566-0001
202-416-8845
fax: 202-416-8802
http://kennedy-
center.org/learn/html/kcaaen.html

National Art Education Association
1916 Association Drive
Reston, VA 20191-1590
703-860-8000
http://www.naea-reston.org

National Association for
Community Education
3929 Old Lee Highway, Suite 91-A
Fairfax, VA 22030-2401
703-359-8973
fax: 703-359-0972

National Building Museum
401 F Street, NW
Washington, DC 20001
202-272-2448
http://www.nbm.org

National Center for Improving
Science Education
2000 L Street, NW, Suite 603
Washington, DC 20036
202-467-0652
fax: 202-467-0659
e-mail: info@ncise.org

National Center on Education
and the Economy
New Standards
700 11th Street, NW, Suite 750
Washington, DC 20001
202-783-3668
fax: 202-783-3672
e-mail: info@ncee.org
http://www.ncee.org

National Council for Geographic
Education
16-A Leonard Hall
Indiana University of Pennsylvania
Indiana, PA 15705-1087
412-357-6290
http://multimedia2.freac.fsu.edu/ncge

National Council for the Social Studies
3501 Newark Street, NW
Washington, DC 20016
202-966-7840
http://www.ncss.org/home/ncss

National Council of Teachers of English
1111 West Kenyon Road
Urbana, IL 61801
1-800-369-6283
http://www.ncte.org

National Council of
Teachers of Mathematics
1906 Association Drive
Reston, VA 20191-1593
703-620-9840
http://www.nctm.org

National Endowment for the Arts,
Education and Access Division
1100 Pennsylvania Avenue, NW, Room 702
Washington, DC 20506
202-682-5438
fax: 202-682-5002 or 5612
http://arts.endow.gov

National Science Teachers Association
1840 Wilson Boulevard
Arlington, VA 22201
703-243-7100
http://www.nsta.org

National Trust for Historic Preservation
1785 Massachusetts Avenue, NW
Washington, DC 20036
202-588-6164
e-mail: response@nthp.org
http://www.nthp.org

North American Association for
Environmental Education
1255 23rd Street, NW, Suite 400
Washington, DC 20037
202-884-8912
fax: 202-884-8701
http://eelink.umich.edu/naaee.html

Package Design Council
481 Carlisle Drive
Herndon, VA 20170
703-318-7225
fax: 703-318-0310
http://www.packinfo-world.org

President's Council on
Sustainable Development
730 Jackson Place, NW
Washington, DC 20503
202-408-5296
fax: 202-408-6839
http://www.whitehouse.gov/PCSD

Project UPDATE and TIES Magazine
Department of Technological Studies
The College of New Jersey
103 Armstrong Hall
Trenton, NJ 08650-4700
609-771-3333
fax: 609-771-3330
http://www.tcnj.edu/teched

Quill and Scroll Society
School of Journalism and Mass
Communication,
University of Iowa
Iowa City, IA 52242
319-335-5795
e-mail: quill-scroll@uiowa.edu
http://www.uiowa.edu/~quill-sc

Salvadori Educational Center on the Built
Environment CCNY
138th St. and Convent Avenue, Room 202
New York, NY 10031
212-650-5497
fax: 212-650-5546

**Scholastic Art and Writing Awards
(design awards)**
Alliance for Young Artists & Writers, Inc.
555 Broadway
New York, NY 10012-3999
212-343-6891
fax: 212-343-6484

School Zone Institute, College of
Architecture and Planning
University of New Mexico
2414 Central, SE
Albuquerque, NM 87131
505-277-5058
fax: 505-277-7113

Second Nature
44 Bromfield Street, 5th Floor
Boston, MA 02108
617-292-7771
fax: 617-292-0150
http://www.2nature.org

**SIGGRAPH (Special Interest Group
on Computer Graphics)**
Association for Computing Machinery
1515 Broadway
New York, NY 10036
212-626-0500
http://www.siggraph.org

Society for Environmental Graphic Design
401 F Street, NW, Suite 333
Washington, DC 20001
202-638-5555
fax: 202-638-0891
e-mail: SEGDOffice@aol.com

Society of Newspaper Design
129 Dyer Street
Providence, RI 02903
401-276-2100
e-mail: snd@snd.org
http://www.snd.org

Urban Land Institute
1025 Thomas Jefferson Street, NW
Suite 500 West
Washington, DC 20007-5201
202-624-7000
fax: 202-624-7140
http://www.uli.org

The Urban Network, College of
Architecture & Urban Planning
3021 Art & Architecture Building
University of Michigan
Ann Arbor, MI 48109-2069
313-936-0201
fax: 313-763-2322
e-mail: sesut@umich.edu

Ventures in Education (Architectural
Youth Program)
245 Fifth Avenue, Suite 802
New York, NY 10016
212-696-5717
fax: 212-696-5726

Worldesign Foundation
186 W. 80th Street
New York, NY 10024
212-769-0330
fax: 212-769-9954

Other Sources
Design and Technology Association
(Journal of Design and Technology)
16 Wellesbourne House,
Walton Road Wellesbourne, Warwickshire
CV35 9JB, England
1789-470-007
fax: 1789-841-955
e-mail: data@dandt.demon.co.uk

Design Dimension Educational Trust
Dean Clough, Halifax HX3 5AX England
1422-250-250
fax: 1422-341-148
e-mail: linda@design-dimension.co.uk

Goldsmiths College, University of London
Design Studies Department,
Technology Education Research Unit
13 Laurie Grove, New Cross
London SE14 6NH
0171-919-7788
fax: 0171-919-7783

IDATER, International Conference
on Design and Technology Educational
Research and Curriculum Development
(see address for Loughborough University below)
1509-222-644
fax: 1509-223-999
e-mail: E.Harvard-Williams@lboro.ac.uk
http://www.lboro.ac.uk/departments/ed/

International Institute
for Information Design
Joergerstrasse 22/2
A/1170 Vienna, Austria
43-1-403-6662
fax: 43-1-408-8347
e-mail: ps.id@magnet.at

Loughborough University
Department of Design and Technology
Loughborough, Leicestershire
LE11 3TU, England
1509-222-650
fax: 1509-223-999
e-mail: P.H.Roberts@lboro.ac.uk
http://www.lboro.ac.uk/departments/cd

SCHOOLS
Cited in this Study

Atwood-Tapleq School *Oakland, Maine**

Banksville Gifted Center *Pittsburgh, Pennsylvania**

Beacon Heights Elementary School *Salt Lake City, Utah*

Beaver Acres School *Beaverton, Oregon**

BEES, Inc. Schools *New Jersey*

  Granville Academy

  Hun School

  Hunterdon Central Regional High School

  Trenton Central High School

Bogle Junior High School *Chandler, Arizona*

Cape Henlopen High School *Lewes, Delaware**

Crossroads High School *Santa Monica, California**

Daniel Webster Magnet School *New Rochelle, New York**

Derby Middle School *Birmingham, Michigan*

Dranesville Elementary School *Herndon, Virginia***

Dyker Heights Intermediate School *Brooklyn, New York***

Eagle Ridge Junior High School *Savage, Minnesota**

El Modena High School *Orange, California**

Epiphany School *Seattle, Washington***

Ethical Culture School *New York, New York**

Fillmore Central School *Fillmore, New York**

Gaithersburg Intermediate School *Gaithersburg, Maryland**

Glasgow High School *Newark, Delaware**

Greenwich High School *Greenwich, Connecticut*

Haggard Middle School *Plano, Texas*

Hawthorne Elementary School *Madison, Wisconsin**

Hawthorne Elementary School *Salt Lake City, Utah*

Hillside High School *Durham, North Carolina*

Holland Christian Middle School *Holland, Michigan**

Institute for Research on Learning *Menlo Park, California***

Lakeview High School *Columbus, Nebraska*

Lincoln High School *Philadelphia, Pennsylvania**

Locust Valley Intermediate School *Locust Valley, New York**

Louis Armstrong Middle School *East Elmhurst, New York**

Marlton Middle School *Marlton, New Jersey**

Meadowthorpe Elementary School *Lexington, Kentucky***

Oak Harbor High School *Oak Harbor, Ohio**

Open Charter Magnet School *Los Angeles, California***

Public School 145 *New York, New York**

Rice Lake Middle School *Rice Lake, Wisconsin**

Sam Houston High School *Lake Charles, Louisiana**

San Jose Middle School *Novato, California***

Sequoyah Middle School *Broken Arrow, Oklahoma**

Simsbury High School *Simsbury, Connecticut**

Smoky Hill High School *Aurora, Colorado***

Soledad Canyon Elementary School *Canyon Country, California**

Special Education Learning Center *Hartford, Connecticut**

Stilwell Elementary School *Kansas City, Kansas**

Tippecanoe Elementary School for the Humanities *Milwaukee, Wisconsin***

Union Grove High School *Union Grove, Wisconsin**

Warren County Middle School *Warren County, North Carolina*

Willamette Primary School *West Linn, Oregon***

Willis Intermediate School *Delaware, Ohio***

* Respondents to Endowment survey
** Respondents to Endowment survey and site-visit school

Bibliography

Books on design for young readers:

Adam, R. (1995). *Buildings: How They Work.* New York: Sterling Publishing Company.

Bender, L. (1991). *Invention.* New York: Alfred A. Knopf, Inc.

Boring, M. (1985). *Incredible Constructions and the People Who Built Them.* New York: Walker and Company.

Brand, S. (1994). *How Buildings Learn: What Happens After They're Built.* New York: Viking Press.

Brown, D. J. (1992). *How Things Were Built.* New York: Random House Books.

D'Alelio, J. (1989). *I Know that Building.* Washington, D.C.: Preservation Press.

Dorros, A. (1992). *This is My House.* New York: Scholastic.

Galla, P. (1995). *How Cities Work.* Emeryville, California: Ziff Davis Press.

Gaughenbaugh, M. and Camburn, H. (1993). *Old House, New House: A Child's Exploration of American Architectural Styles.* Washington, D.C.: Preservation Press.

Gay, K. (1986). *Ergonomics: Making Products and Places Fit People.* Hillside, New Jersey: Enslow Publishing.

Gibbons, G. (1986). *Up Goes the Skyscraper!* New York: Scholastic.

Gibbons, G. (1991). *How a House is Built.* New York: Scholastic.

Giblin, J.C. (1993). *Be Seated: A Book About Chairs.* New York: Harper Collins.

Glenn, P.B. (1996). *Discover America's Favorite Architects.* New York: Preservation Press, John Wiley & Sons, Inc.

Glenn, P.B. (1993). *Under Every Roof: A Kid's Style and Field Guide to the Architecture of American Houses.* Washington, D.C.: Preservation Press.

Hawkes, N. (1993). *Structures: The Way Things Are Built.* New York: Macmillan.

Hellman, L. (1988). *Architecture for Beginners.* New York: Writers and Readers Publishing.

Lewis, B. (1991). *A Kid's Guide to Social Action.* Minneapolis, Minnesota: Free Spirit Publishing.

Isaacson, P. (1990). *Round Buildings, Square Buildings, and Buildings that Wiggle Like a Fish.* New York: Alfred A. Knopf, Inc.

Macaulay, D. (1975). *City, A Story of Roman Planning and Construction.* Boston, Massachusetts: Houghton-Mifflin.

Macaulay, D. (1975). *Pyramid.* Boston, Massachusetts: Houghton-Mifflin.

Macaulay, D. (1976). *Underground.* Boston, Massachusetts: Houghton-Mifflin.

Macaulay, D. (1978). *Great Moments in Architecture.* Boston, Massachusetts: Houghton-Mifflin.

Macaulay, D. (1981). *Cathedral, The Story of Its Construction.* Boston, Massachusetts: Houghton-Mifflin.

Macaulay, D. (1987). *Unbuilding.* Boston, Massachusetts: Houghton-Mifflin.

Macaulay, D. (1988). *The Way Things Work.* Boston, Massachusetts: Houghton-Mifflin. (interactive media, 1994)

Purcell, J. (1982). *From Hand Ax to Laser.* New York: Vanguard Press.

Salvadori, M. (1990). *The Art of Construction.* Chicago, Illinois: Chicago Review Press.

Seltzer, I. (1992). *The House I Live In: A Home in America.* New York: Macmillan.

Thorne-Thomsen, K. (1994). *Frank Lloyd Wright for Kids.* Chicago, Illinois: Chicago Review Press.

Von Tscharner, R. and Fleming, R.L. (1992). *New Providence: A Changing Cityscape.* Washington, D.C.: Preservation Press.

Weiss, H. (1986). *Shelters: From Teepee to Igloo.* New York: Harper Collins.

Weitzman, D. (1982). *Windmills, Bridges, and Old Machines: Discovering Our Industrial Past.* New York: Charles Scribner's Sons.

Whyte, W. (1990). *City: Rediscovering the Center.* New York: Doubleday.

Wilson, F. (1988). *What It Feels Like to Be a Building.* Washington, D.C.: Preservation Press.

Books about design and designing:

Baldwin, J. (1996). *Bucky Works: Buckminster Fuller's Ideas for Today.* New York: John Wiley & Sons.

Blumenson, J. L. (1990). *Identifying American Architecture.* New York: W.W. Norton and Company.

Brand, S. (1994). *How Buildings Learn: What Happens After They're Built.* New York: Viking Press.

Burden, I., Morrison, J., and Twyford, J. (1988). *Design and Designing.* Harlow, Essex England: Longman.

Burke, J. (1980). *Connections.* Boston, Massachusetts: Little, Brown, and Co.

Clay, G. (1995). *Real Places: An Unconventional Guide to America's Generic Landscape.* Chicago, Illinois: University of Chicago Press.

Cullen, G. (1961). *Townscape.* New York: Van Nostrand Reinhold.

Dormer, P. (1993). *Design Since 1945.* New York: Thames and Hudson.

Dreyfuss, H. (1967). *Designing for People.* New York: Grossman Publishers.

Forty, A. (1986). *Objects of Desire: Design and Society from Wedgwood to IBM.* New York: Pantheon Books.

Friedman, M. and Freshman, P. (1989). *Graphic Design in America: A Visual Language History.* New York: Harry N. Abrams, Inc.

Hale, J. (1994). *The Old Way of Seeing.* New York: Houghton-Mifflin.

Hall, E.T. (1959). *Silent Language.* New York: Doubleday.

Hall, E.T. (1966). *The Hidden Dimension.* New York: Doubleday.

Hiebert, K. J. (1992). *Graphic Design Processes.* New York: Van Nostrand Reinhold.

Hoffman, A. (1965). *Graphic Design Manual: Principles and Practice.* New York: Van Nostrand Reinhold.

Jackson, J.B. (1994). *A Sense of Place, A Sense of Time.* New Haven, Connecticut: Yale University Press.

Jackson, D.C. (1988). *Great American Bridges and Dams.* Washington, D.C.: The Preservation Press.

Jones, J.C. (1970). *Design Methods.* New York: Wiley-Interscience.

Kostof, S. (1987). *American by Design.* New York: Oxford University Press.

Lawson, B. (1990). *How Designers Think: The Design Process Demystified,* 2nd edition. Oxford, England: Butterworth-Architecture.

Lewis, R.K. (1985). *Master Builders: A Guide to Famous American Architects.* Washington, D.C.: Preservation Press.

Liebs, C.H. (1995). *Main Street to Miracle Mile: American Roadside Architecture.* Baltimore, Maryland: Johns Hopkins University Press.

Livingston, A. and Livingston, I. (1992). *Encyclopedia of Graphic Design and Designers.* London, England: Thames and Hudson.

Lynch, K. (1988). *The Image of the City.* Boston, Massachusetts: MIT Press.

Meggs, P. (1983). *The History of Graphic Design.* New York: Van Nostrand Reinhold.

Morgan, J. and Welton, P. (1992). *See What I Mean? An Introduction to Visual Communication.* New York: Routledge, Chapman, and Hall.

Norman, D. (1986). *The Design of Everyday Things.* New York: Doubleday.

Norman, D. (1993). *Things that Make Us Smart: Defending Human Attributes in the Age of the Machine.* New York: Addison-Wesley Publishing Company.

Petroski, H. (1992). *The Evolution of Useful Things.* New York: Alfred A. Knopf, Inc.

Petroski, H. (1992). *The Pencil: A History of Design and Circumstance.* New York: Alfred A. Knopf, Inc.

Pile, J.F. (1979). *Design: Purpose, Form and Meaning.* New York: W.W. Norton and Company.

Pile, J.F. (1994). *The Dictionary of 20th Century Design.* New York: DaCapo Press.

Poppeliers, J. (1984). *What is Style? A Guide to American Architecture.* Washington, D.C.: Preservation Press.

Pulos, A. (1988). *The American Design Adventure.* Boston, Massachusetts: MIT Press.

Rasmussen, S. (1962). *Experiencing Architecture.* Boston, Massachusetts: MIT Press.

Salvadori, M. (1986). *Structure in Architecture: The Building of Buildings.* Englewood Cliffs, New Jersey: Prentice-Hall.

Salvadori, M. (1990). *Why Buildings Stand Up: The Strength of Architecture.* New York: W.W. Norton and Company.

Salvadori, M. and Levy, M. (1992). *Why Buildings Fall Down: How Structures Fail.* New York: W.W. Norton and Company.

Savage, B.L. (1994). *African American Historic Places.* New York: John Wiley & Sons.

Simon, H. (1969). *The Sciences of the Artificial.* Cambridge, Massachusetts: MIT Press.

Sommer, R. (1972). *Design Awareness.* Fort Worth, Texas: Rinehart Press.

Sommer, R. (1983). *Social Design: Creating Buildings with People In Mind.* Englewood Cliffs, New Jersey: Prentice Hall.

Sparke, P. (1986). *An Introduction to Design and Culture in the Twentieth Century.* New York: Allen and Unwin.

Sparke, P. (1987). *Design in Context.* New York: Chartwell Books.

Tishler, W.H., ed. (1989). *American Landscape Architecture: Designers and Places.* Washington, D.C.: Preservation Press.

Tufte, E. (1990). *Envisioning Information.* Cheshire, Connecticut: Graphics Press.

Upton, D., ed. (1987). *America's Architectural Roots: Ethnic Groups that Built America.* Washington, D.C.: Preservation Press.

Wurman, R.S. (1972). *The Nature of Recreation.* Boston, Massachusetts: MIT Press.

Wurman, R.S. (1989). *Information Anxiety.* New York: Doubleday.

Books about contemporary environmental issues in design:

Arendt, R.G. (1996). *Conservation Design for Subdivisions: A Practical Guide to Creating Open Space Networks.* Washington, D.C.: Island Press.

Cairncross, F. (1995). *Green, Inc., A Guide to Business and the Environment.* Washington, D.C.: Island Press.

Carlson, D. (1995). *At Road's End: Transportation and Land Use Choices for Communities.* Washington, D.C.: Island Press.

Davis, S. (1995). *The Architecture of Affordable Housing.* Berkeley, California: University of California Press.

Diamond, H.L. and Noonan, P. (1996). *Land Use in America.* Washington, D.C.: Island Press.

Garvin, A. (1995). *The American City: What Works, What Doesn't.* New York: McGraw-Hill.

Geddes, R., ed. (1996). *Cities in Our Future.* Washington, D.C.: Island Press.

Goldstein, J.B. and Elliott, C.D. (1994). *Designing America: Creating Urban Identity.* New York: Van Nostrand Reinhold.

Hiss, T. (1990). *The Experience of Place.* New York: Alfred A. Knopf, Inc.

Kunstler, J.H. (1993). *The Geography of Nowhere: The Rise and Fall of America's Man-Made Landscape.* New York: Simon and Schuster.

Lewis, P.H., Jr. (1996). *Tomorrow by Design: A Regional Design Process for Sustainability.* New York: John Wiley & Sons.

Lyle, J. T. (1996). *Regenerative Design for Sustainable Development.* New York: John Wiley & Sons.

McHarg, I. (1995). *Design with Nature.* New York: John Wiley & Sons.

Orr, D. (1994). *Earth in Mind: On Education, Environment, and the Human Prospect.* Washington, D.C.: Island Press.

Papanek, V. (1985). *Design for the Real World: Human Ecology and Social Change,* 2nd edition. New York: Van Nostrand Reinhold.

Porter, D. (1997). *Managing Growth in America's Communities.* Washington, D.C.: Island Press.

President's Council on Sustainable Development (1996). *Sustainable America: A New Consensus for Prosperity, Opportunity, and a Healthy Environment for the Future.* Washington, D.C.: President's Council on Sustainable Development.

Steiner, F. (1990). *The Living Landscape.* New York: McGraw-Hill.

Van der Ryn, S. and Calthorpe, P. (1991). *Sustainable Communities: A New Design Synthesis for Cities, Suburbs, and Towns.* San Francisco, California: Sierra Club Books.

Van der Ryn, S. and Cowen, S. (1996). *Ecological Design.* Washington, D.C.: Island Press.

Whitaker, C. (1996). *Architecture and the American Dream.* New York: Clarkson N. Potter Publishers.

Zeiher, L.C. *The Ecology of Architecture: A Complete Guide to Creating the Environmentally Conscious Building.* New York: Watson-Guptill Publications.

Books about teaching and learning through design:

Adams, E. (1982). *Art and the Built Environment.* London, England: Longman.

Archer, B., Baynes, K., and Roberts, P. (1992). *The Nature of Research into Design and Technology Education.* Loughborough, England: Loughborough University.

Baynes, K. (1992). *Children Designing.* Loughborough, England: Department of Design and Technology, Loughborough University.

Baynes, K. (1994). *Designerly Play.* Loughborough, England: Department of Design and Technology, Loughborough University.

Baynes, K. (1996). *How Children Choose: Children's Encounters with Design.* Loughborough, England: Department of Design and Technology, Loughborough University.

Bones, D., ed. (1994). *Getting Started: A Guide to Bringing Environmental Education into Your Classroom.* Ann Arbor, Michigan: National Consortium for Environmental Education and Training, University of Michigan.

Bottrill, P. (1995). *Designing and Learning in the Elementary School.* Reston, Virginia: International Technology Education Association.

Burnette, C. and Norman, J. (1997). *DK-12: Design for Thinking.* Tucson, Arizona: Crizmac.

Center for Civic Education (1996). *We the People...Project Citizen.* Calabasas, California: Center for Civic Education.

Copeland, R., Abhau, M., and Greenberg, G., eds. (1986). *Architecture in Education.* Philadelphia, Pennsylvania: Foundation for Architecture.

Davis, M. and Moore, R. (1992). *Education through Design: The Middle School Curriculum.* Raleigh, North Carolina: School of Design/North Carolina State University.

D'Alelio, J. (1989). *I Know that Building: Discovering Architecture with Activities and Games.* Washington, D.C.: Preservation Press.

DeBono, E. (1972). *Children Solve Problems.* New York: Penguin Books.

DeVore, P. (1989). *Design and Technology.* Worcester, Massachusetts: Davis Publishing.

Dunn, S. and Larson, R. (1990). *Design Technology: Children's Engineering.* Bristol, Pennsylvania: Falmer Press.

Eggleston, J. (1996). *Teaching Design and Technology.* Philadelphia, Pennsylvania: Open University Press.

Eriksen, A. and Wintermute, M. (1983). *Students, Structures, Spaces: Activities in the Built Environment.* Reading, Massachusetts: Addison-Wesley Publishing Company.

Farrell, A. and Patterson, J. (1993). *Understanding Assessment in Design and Technology.* London, England: Hodder and Stoughton.

Garratt, J. (1991). *Design and Technology.* New York: Cambridge University Press.

Gordon, W.J.J. (1973). *The Metaphorical Way of Knowing and Learning.* Cambridge, Massachusetts: Porpoise Books.

Graves, G. (1997). *Walk Around the Block.* Prairie Village, Kansas: Center for Understanding the Built Environment.

Hanks, K., Belliston, L., and Edwards, D. (1991). *Design Yourself.* Los Altos, California: Crisp Publications.

Hart, R.A. (1997). *Children's Participation: The Theory and Practice of Involving Young Citizens in Community Development and Environmental Care.* London, England: Earthscan Publications, Ltd.

Hubel, V. and Lussow, D. (1984). *Focus on Designing.* New York: McGraw-Hill.

Jinks, D. and Williams, P. (1991). *Design and Technology.* 5-12. Bristol, Pennsylvania: Falmer Press.

Kasprisin, R. and Pettinari, J. (1995). *Visual Thinking for Architects and Designers: Visualizing Context in Design.* New York: Van Nostrand Reinhold.

Kimbell, R., Stables, K., and Green, R. (1996). *Understanding Practice in Design and Technology.* Philadelphia, Pennsylvania: Open University Press.

Layton, D. (1992). *Values and Design and Technology.* Loughborough, England: Department of Design and Technology, Loughborough University.

Layton, D. (1993). *Technology's Challenge to Science Education.* Philadelphia, Pennsylvania: Open University Press.

Layton, D., ed. (1994). *Innovations in Science and Technology Education.* Paris, France: UNESCO Publications, 1994.

Lewis, B. (1991). *A Kid's Guide to Social Action.* Minneapolis, Minnesota: Free Spirit Publishing.

McKim, R.H. (1979). *Experiences in Visual Thinking.* Monterey, California: Brooks/Cole Publishing.

McKim, R. H. (1980). *Thinking Visually: A Strategy Manual for Problem Solving.* Belmont, California: Lifetime Learning Publications.

Mitchell, A. and David, J., eds. (1992). *Explorations with Young Children: A Curriculum Guide from the Bank Street College of Education.* Mt. Ranier, Michigan: Gryphon House.

Moore, R. and Wong, H.H. (1997). *Natural Learning: The Story of an Environmental Schoolyard.* Berkeley, California: MIG Communications.

Mullahey, R. (1994). *Community As a Learning Resource.* Chicago, Illinois: Planners Book Service.

Nelson, D. (1982). *Manual for City Building Education Project.* Los Angeles, California: Center for City Building Education.

Nelson, D. (1984). *Transformations: Process and Theory.* Los Angeles, California: Center for Building Education Programs.

Olsen, G. and Olsen, M. (1985). *Archi-Teacher: A Guide to Architecture in the Schools.* Champaign, Illinois: Educational Concepts Group.

Pollard, J. (1988). *Building Toothpick Bridges.* Palo Alto, California: Dale Seymour Publications.

Raizen, S., Sellwood, P., Todd, R., and Vickers, M. (1995). *Technology Education in the Classroom: Understanding the Designed World.* San Francisco, California: Jossey-Bass Publishers, Inc.

Roberts, P., Archer, B., and Baynes, K. (1992) *Modelling: The Language of Designing.* Loughborough, England: Department of Design and Technology, Loughborough University.

Roukes, N. (1988). *Design Synectics: Stimulating Creativity in Design.* Worcester, Massachusetts: Davis Publications.

Royal College of Art (1976). *Design in General Education, Part One, Summary of Findings and Recommendations.* London, England: Royal College of Art.

Salvadori, M. (1993). *Architecture and Engineering: An Illustrated Teacher's Manual on Why Buildings Stand Up.* New York: New York Academy of Sciences.

Sandler, A.R., ed. (1988). *The Source Book II, Learning by Design.* Washington, D.C.: The American Institute of Architects Press.

Shadrin, R.L. (1993). *Design & Drawing, An Applied Approach.* Worcester, Massachusetts: Davis Publishing.

Slafer, A. and Cahill, K. (1995). *Why Design?* Chicago, Illinois: Chicago Review Press.

Stine, S. (1997). *Landscapes for Learning: Creating Outdoor Environments for Children and Youth.* New York: John Wiley & Sons.

Sutton, S. (undated). *The Urban Network Instructional Portfolio: An Urban Design Program for Elementary Schools.* Ann Arbor, Michigan: University of Michigan.

Taylor, A. (1991). *Architecture and Children: Learning by Design, Teachers Guide and Poster Sets.* Albuquerque, New Mexico: American Institute of Architects.

Thistlewood, D., ed. (1990). *Issues in Design Education.* New York: Longman.

Tickle, L. (1990). *Craft, Design and Technology in Primary School Classrooms.* Bristol, Pennsylvania: Taylor and Francis Publishers (Falmer Press).

Todd, R., Todd, K., and McCrory, D. (1995). *Introduction to Design and Technology.* Cincinnati, Ohio: Southwestern.

Tufnell, R. (1986). *Design and Communication.* London, England: Hutchinson.

Urban Land Institute. (1990). *Dilemmas of Development.* Washington, D.C.: Urban Land Institute.

Urban Land Institute. (1991). *Urban Plan: A High School Teaching Unit.* Washington, D.C.: Urban Land Institute.

Von Wodtke, M. (1992). *Mind Over Media: Creative Thinking Skills for Electronic Media.* New York: McGraw-Hill.

Weber, R.J. (1993). *Forks, Phonographs, and Hot Air Balloons: A Field Guide to Inventive Thinking.* London, England: Oxford University Press.

Welch, P., ed. (1995). *Strategies for Teaching Universal Design.* Boston, Massachusetts: Adaptive Environments Center.

Winters, N.B. (1986). *Architecture is Elementary: Visual Thinking Through Architectural Concepts.* Napoleon, Ohio: Gibbs Smith Publisher.

Books about learning, curriculum, pedagogy, and assessment:

Armstrong, T. (1992). *Seven Kinds of Smart: Identifying and Developing Your Many Intelligences.* New York: Plume.

Belanoff, P. and Dickson, M., eds. (1991). *Portfolios: Process and Product.* New York: Heinemann, Boyton, Cook.

Boughton, D., Eisner, E., and Ligtvoet, J. (1996). *Evaluating and Assessing the Visual Arts in Education: International Perspectives.* New York: Teachers College Press.

De Bono, E. (1990). *Lateral Thinking: Creativity Step by Step.* Mamaroneck, New York: International Center for Creative Thinking.

Brooks, M. and Brooks, J. (1993). *In Search of Understanding: The Case for Constructivist Classrooms.* Alexandria, Virginia: Association for Supervision and Curriculum Development.

Bruner, J. (1979). *On Knowing: Essays for the Left Hand.* Cambridge, Massachusetts: Belknap Press.

Condry, J. (1978). "The Role of Incentives in Socialization." In *The Hidden Cost of Rewards.* Green, D. and Lepper, M.R., eds. Hillsdale, New Jersey: Lawrence Erlbaum Associates.

Deci, E. and Ryan, R. (1991). *Intrinsic Motivation and Self-Determination in Human Behavior.* New York: Plenum Press.

Deci, E., Ryan, R.M., and Connell, J.P. (1985). "A Motivational Analysis of Self-determination and Self-regulation in Education." In *Research on Motivation in Education: The Classroom Milieu,* Volume 2. Ames, C. and Ames, R., eds. New York: Academic Press.

Dewey, J. (1902). *The Child and the Curriculum.* Chicago, Illinois: University of Chicago Press.

Dewey, J. (1910). *My Pedagogic Creed.* Chicago, Illinois: A. Flanagan Company.

Dewey, J. (1938). *Experiences and Education.* New York: Macmillan.

Dunn, R. and Dunn, K. (1978). *Teaching Students Through Their Individual Learning Styles: A Practical Approach.* Englewood Cliffs, New Jersey: Prentice Hall.

Edwards, B. (1988). *Drawing on the Right Side of the Brain.* New York: St. Martin's Press.

Gardner, H. (1983). *Frames of Mind: Theories of Multiple Intelligences.* New York: Basic Books.

Gardner, H. (1990). *Art Education and Human Development.* Los Angeles, California: Getty Center for Education in the Arts.

Gardner, H. (1990). *Art, Mind, and Brain: A Cognitive Approach to Creativity.* New York: Basic Books.

Gardner, H. (1991). *The Unschooled Mind: How Children Think and How Schools Should Teach.* New York: Basic Books.

Gardner, H. (1993). *Multiple Intelligences: The Theory and Practice.* New York: Basic Books.

Healy, J. (1991). *Endangered Minds: Why Our Children Don't Think, and What We Can Do about It.* New York: Simon and Schuster.

Hodgkin, R. (1985). *Playing and Exploring: Education through the Discovery of Order.* New York: Methune Publishers.

Huckle, J. and Sterling, S., eds. (1996). *Education for Sustainability.* London, England: Earthscan Publications, Ltd.

Hyerle, D. (1989). *Knowledge Acquisition from Text and Pictures.* New York: North Holland.

Hyerle, D. (1996). *Visual Tools for Constructing Knowledge.* Alexandria, Virginia: Association for Supervision and Curriculum Development.

Jacobs, H.H. (1989). *Interdisciplinary Curriculum: Design and Implementation.* Alexandria, Virginia: Association for Supervision and Curriculum Development.

Johnson, D., Johnson, R., and Holubec, E.J. (1994). *The New Circles of Learning: Cooperation in the Classroom and School.* Alexandria, Virginia: Association for Supervision and Curriculum Development.

Kimbell, R., Stables, K., Wheeler, T., Wosniak, A., and Vickers, K. (1991). *The Assessment of Performance in Design and Technology.* London, England: School Examinations and Assessment Council.

Massell, D., Fuhrman, S., Kirst, M., Odden, A., Wohlstetter, P., Carver, R., and Yee, G. (1993). *Ten Years of State Education Reform, 1983-1993.* New Brunswick, New Jersey: Consortium for Policy Research in Education.

Nickerson, R., Perkins, D., and Smith, E. (1985). *The Teaching of Thinking.* Hillsdale, New Jersey: Erlbaum Associates.

Papert, S. (1993). *The Children's Machine, Bringing the Computer Revolution to Our Schools.* New York: Basic Books.

Perkins, D. (1977). *The Arts and Cognition.* Baltimore, Maryland: Johns Hopkins University Press.

Perkins, D. (1981). *The Mind's Best Work.* Cambridge, Massachusetts: Harvard University Press.

Perkins, D. (1986). *Knowledge As Design*. Hillsdale, New Jersey: Lawrence Erlbaum Associates.

Perkins, D. (1992). *Inventive Minds: Creativity in Technology*. London, England: Oxford University Press.

Perkins, D. (1992). *Smart Schools: Better Thinking and Learning for Every Child*. New York: Free Press.

Perkins, D. (1994). *The Intelligent Eye: Learning to Think by Looking at Art*. Los Angeles, California: Getty Center for Education in the Arts.

Perkins, D. (1995). *Software Goes to School, Teaching for Understanding with New Technologies*. New York: Oxford University Press.

Perkins, D. and Tishman, S. (1995). *The Thinking Classroom: Learning and Teaching in a Culture of Thinking*. Needham Heights, Massachusetts: Allyn and Bacon.

Resnick, L., ed. (1987). *Education and Learning to Think*. Washington, D.C.: National Research Council, National Academy Press.

Samples, B. (1976). *The Metaphoric Mind*. Reading, Massachusetts: Addison-Wesley.

Samples, B. (1987). *Open Mind/Whole Mind*. Rolling Estates, California: Jalmar Press.

Schaefer, J. (1995). *Sight Unseen: The Art of Active Seeing*. Glenview, Illinois: Good Year Books.

Siegler, R. (1989). *How Children Discover New Strategies*. Hillsdale, New Jersey: Lawrence Erlbaum Associates.

Slavin, R. (1986). *Using Student Team Learning, The Johns Hopkins Team Learning Project*. Baltimore, Maryland: Center for Research on Elementary and Middle Schools.

Sternberg, R. (1988). *The Nature of Creativity*. Cambridge, England: Cambridge University Press.

Sternberg, R. (1991). *Complex Problem Solving*. Hillsdale, New Jersey: Lawrence Erlbaum Associates.

Sternberg, R. (1994). *Thinking and Problem Solving*. New York: Academic Press.

Sternberg, R. (1995). *Defying the Crowd: Cultivating Creativity in a Culture of Conformity*. New York: Free Press.

Sternberg, R. (1995). *The Nature of Insight*. Boston, Massachusetts: MIT Press.

Sternberg, R. and Baron, J.B. (1987). *Teaching Thinking Skills: Theory and Practice*. New York: W.H. Freeman.

Vickers, M., ed. (1995). *Integrating Social Studies, Economics, Language Arts and Workplace Learning*. Andover, Massachusetts: The NETWORK, Inc.

Wolf, D.P. (1996). *Performance-Based Student Assessment: Challenges and Possibilities*. Chicago, Illinois: University of Chicago Press.

Books on education reform:

Arias-La Forgia, A. (1994). *Environmental Education in the School Systems of Latin America and the Caribbean*, Working Papers, No. 4. Washington, D.C.: Academy for Educational Development for the Education and Human Resources Division, Bureau for Latin America and the Caribbean, U.S. Agency for International Development.

American Association for the Advancement of Science, Project 2061. (1989). *Science for All Americans*. New York: Oxford University Press.

American Association for the Advancement of Science, Project 2061. (1993). *Benchmarks for Science Literacy*. New York: Oxford University Press.

American Association for the Advancement of Science, Project 2061. (1997). *Designs for Science Literacy*. Washington, D.C.: American Association for the Advancement of Science.

Black, P. and Atkin, J.M. (1996). *Changing the Subject: Innovations in Science, Mathematics, and Technology Education.* New York: Routledge, with the Organization for Economic Cooperation and Development, Paris, France.

Business Task Force on Student Standards. (1995). *The Challenge of Change: Standards to Make Education Work for All Our Children.* Washington, D.C.: Business Coalition for Education Reform.

Center for Civic Education. (1994). *National Standards for Civics and Government.* Calabasas, California: Center for Civic Education.

Consortium of National Art Education Associations. (1994). *National Standards for Art Education: What Every Young American Should Know and Be Able to Do in the Arts.* Reston, Virginia: Music Educators National Conference.

Cowley, T. and Williamson, J. (1995). *OECD Report on Science, Mathematics, and Technology in Education (SMTE) Project.* Launceston, Tasmania: University of Tasmania, School of Education.

Education for Sustainability Working Group. (1996). *Education for Sustainability: An Agenda for Action.* Washington, D.C.: President's Council on Sustainable Development.

Edwards, C., Gandini, L., and Forman, G., eds. (1993). *The Hundred Languages of Children: The Reggio Emilia Approach to Early Childhood Education.* Norwood, New Jersey: Ablex Publishing Corporation.

Franssen, H.A.M., Eijkelhof, H.M.C., Houtveen, A.A.M., and Duijmelinck, H.A.J.P. (1995). *Technology as a School Subject in Junior Secondary School in the Netherlands.* Utrecht, The Netherlands: University of Utrecht, Department of Education.

Geography Education Standards Project. (1994). *Geography for Life: National Geography Standards.* Washington, D.C.: National Geographic Research and Exploration.

Goodlad, J. (1983). *Individual Differences and the Common Curriculum.* Chicago, Illinois: University of Chicago Press and National Society for the Study of Education.

Goodlad, J. (1994). *Educational Renewal: Better Teachers, Better Schools.* San Francisco, California: Jossey-Bass.

Goodlad, J., ed. (1984). *A Place Called School: Prospects for the Future.* New York: McGraw-Hill.

Holmes Group. (1995). *Tomorrow's Schools of Education.* East Lansing, Michigan: Holmes Group.

Kormylo, P. and Frame, J. (1995). *A Report on Technology in Case Study Primary Schools in Scotland.* Edinburgh, Scotland: Scottish Office Education Department.

National Assessment Governing Board. (1994). *NAEP Arts Education Consensus Project, Arts Education Assessment Framework* (Pre-publication edition). Washington, D.C.: The Chief State School Officers with the College Board and the Council for Basic Education.

National Center on Education and the Economy and the University of Pittsburgh. (1997). *Performance Standards, Volume 2, Middle School.* Washington, D.C.: National Center on Education and the Economy.

National Commission on Excellence in Education. (1983). *A Nation at Risk: The Imperative for Educational Reform.* Washington, D.C.: U.S. Government Printing Office.

The National Council on Education Standards and Testing. (1992). *Raising Standards for American Education.* Washington, D.C.: Superintendent of Documents and Government Printing Office.

National Council of Teachers of English and International Reading Association. (1996). *Standards for the English Language Arts.* Urbana, Illinois, and Newark, Delaware: National Council of Teachers of English and International Reading Association.

National Council of Teachers of Mathematics. (1989). *Curriculum and Evaluation Standards for School Mathematics.* Washington, D.C.: Working Groups of the Commission on Standards for School Mathematics of the National Council of Teachers of Mathematics.

National Council for the Social Studies. (1994). *Expectations of Excellence, Curriculum Standards for Social Studies.* Washington, D.C.: National Council for the Social Studies.

National Endowment for the Arts. (1994). *Goals 2000: Opportunities for the Arts.* Washington, D.C.: National Endowment for the Arts, U.S. Department of Education, and National Assembly of State Arts Agencies.

National Environmental Education Advisory Council. (1996 draft). *Report Assessing Environmental Education in the United States.* Washington, D.C.: Environmental Protection Agency.

National Institute for Educational Research. (1993). *Environmental Education and Teacher Education in Asia and the Pacific.* Tokyo, Japan: NIER.

National Research Council and National Academy of Sciences. (1996). *National Science Education Standards.* Washington, D.C.: National Academy Press.

New Standards Project. (1997). *Performance Standards in English Language Arts, Mathematics, Science, and Applied Learning.* Washington, D.C.: National Center on Education and the Economy.

North American Association for Environmental Education. (1997 draft). *Environmental Education Guidelines for Excellence: What School-Age Learners Should Know and Be Able to Do.* Washington, D.C.: North American Association for Environmental Education.

Organization for Economic Cooperation and Development. (1991). *Environment, Schools, and Active Learning.* Paris, France: OECD.

Organization for Economic Cooperation and Development. (1995). *Environmental Learning for the 21st Century.* Paris, France: OECD.

The Secretary's Commission on Achieving Necessary Skills. (1991). *What Work Requires of Schools: A SCANS Report for America 2000.* Washington, D.C.: U.S. Department of Labor.

United States Department of Labor. (1992). *Skills and Tasks for Jobs, A SCANS Report for America 2000.* Washington, D.C.: United States Department of Labor.

United States Department of Labor, Employment and Training Administration. (1987). *Workforce 2000: Work and Workers for the 21st Century.* Washington, D.C.: prepared by the Hudson Institute for the Department of Labor, Superintendent of Documents.

Credits:

We are grateful to the following for providing the photography and artwork that appears throughout this book. We regret that we were unable to publish all of the excellent artwork we received from the many outstanding educators participating in this project.

Penny Archibald-Stone, Autodesk, Brochocka Baynes, Teresa F. Bettac, Lisa Bloomfield, Pauline Bottrill, Steve Brady, Patrick Buechner, Shirl Buss, Pamela Carunchio, Chicago Architecture Foundation, Cooper-Hewitt National Design Museum, Meredith Davis, Susan Dunn, Pete Ellenzweig, Wendy Fein, Will Fowler, Manette Gampel, Ania Greiner, Katie Mead Griffiths, Michael Hacker, Peter Hiller, Historic Landmarks Foundation of Indiana, Paul Hobson, K. Holtgraves, Patricia Hutchinson, Daniel Iacofano, Richard Igneri, Hettie Jordan-Vilanova, Mary Ann Keith, KIDS Consortium, James J. Kirkwood, Stephan Knobloch, Janice Leonetti, Maxis Software, Robin Moore, Doreen Nelson, Julie Olsen, Lynn Olson, Dolores Patton, Brenda Peters, Julie Ritter, Marvin Rosenblum, Jan Rothschild, Anna Sanko, Mark Sokol, Suzanne R. Stanis, Jane Stickney, Jan Striefel, Joseph Sweeney, Anne Taylor, Catherine Teegarden, Terry Thode, Ann Tucker, Ventures in Education, Inc., Yu-Wen Wang, Paula White, Lorraine Whitman, Val Wiebeck, Karen Wintress.

About the Authors

Meredith Davis is Professor of Graphic Design at North Carolina State University where she teaches graduate courses on design and cognition. She is also an author, lecturer, and consultant on the relationship between design and K-12 education. Davis holds an M.F.A. from Cranbrook Academy of Art and a B.S. and M.Ed. in art education from Pennsylvania State University.

Peter Hawley develops public education and partnership projects at the American Planning Association in Washington, D.C. Previously, he directed a number of education initiatives at the Design Program of the National Endowment for the Arts, including Design as a Catalyst for Learning. Hawley holds a master's degree in education from the University of Massachusetts, a master's degree in historic preservation from the University of Vermont and an undergraduate degree in history from Princeton University.

Bernard J. McMullan, Ph.D. has more than 15 years experience in the design and assessment of educational reform strategies with a focus on studying institutional change collaborations at the secondary and post-secondary levels. He has worked with the National Endowment for the Arts and the Mississippi Arts Commission assessing the educational benefits of arts-infused education on student achievement and school improvement.

Gertrude J. Spilka is Associate Director of the OMG Center for Collaborative Learning in Philadelphia where she has directed several research projects that explore the role of the arts in education reform. She is currently directing an assessment of ArtsEdge, a Web site sponsored by the John F. Kennedy Center for the Performing Arts, the National Endowment for the Arts, and the U.S. Department of Education to disseminate information to advance arts education and education reform objectives.

About the NEA

The National Endowment for the Arts

Established by Congress in 1965, the National Endowment for the Arts is an independent agency of the federal government. The Endowment's mission is *to foster the excellence, diversity, and vitality of the arts in the United States, and to broaden public access to the arts.*

The Endowment carries out that mission through grants, leadership initiatives, partnership agreements with state and regional organizations, partnerships with other federal agencies and the private sector, research, arts education, access programs, and advocacy.

Since 1996, the Arts Endowment has considered applications and proposals from eligible individuals and organizations in four ways: grants to organizations, grants to individuals, partnership agreements, and leadership initiatives. Grants to organizations include four categories: Heritage and Preservation, Education and Access, Creation and Presentation, and Planning and Stabilization. Applications are reviewed by rotating groups of arts experts including professional artists, arts educators, arts administrators, and knowledgeable laypersons.

For more information, visit the Endowment online at http://www.arts .endow.gov/ or call 202/682-5400.

The Endowment and Arts Education

Almost from its inception, the Arts Endowment has encouraged and supported efforts to increase opportunities in and improve the quality of arts education for America's children, youth, and adults. Since 1988, when the Endowment published the landmark report on the status of American arts education, *Toward Civilization*, the agency has been particularly committed to making the arts a part of the basic education of every student in grades K to 12.

At the national level, the Arts Endowment in recent years has supported the development of the National Standards for Arts Education, and the 1997 National Assessment of Educational Progress (better known as NAEP or the Nation's Report Card) Arts Assessment. In cooperation with the U.S. Department of Education, the Endowment has supported the Goals 2000 Arts Education Partnership, which is comprised of more than 100 national organizations from the education, arts, business, and government sectors working to ensure a vital role for the arts in state-and local-level educational improvement. For information about the Partnership, call 202/326-8693 or visit the Partnership online at http://artsedge.kennedy-center. org/aep/aep.html/ .

To increase access to information about arts teaching and learning, the Arts Endowment, in partnership with the Department of Education, supports ArtsEdge, an electronic network sponsored by the John F. Kennedy Center for the Performing Arts. ArtsEdge services include arts education news, a Search Lab for access to documents, directories, and resources; and a Curriculum Studio designed to provide teachers and artist-educators with examples of innovative programs and practices. For more information, visit online at http://artsedge.kennedy-center .org/ or call 202/416-8871.

About ASCD

ASCD

Founded in 1943, the Association for Supervision and Curriculum Development is a nonpartisan, nonprofit education association, with international headquarters in Alexandria, Virginia. ASCD's mission statement: *ASCD, a diverse, international community of educators, forging covenants in teaching and learning for the success of all learners.*

Membership in ASCD includes a subscription to the award-winning journal *Educational Leadership*; two newsletters, *Education Update* and *Curriculum Update*; and other products and services. ASCD sponsors affiliate organizations in many states and international locations; participates in collaborations and networks; holds conferences, institutes, and training programs; produces publications in a variety of media; sponsors recognition and awards programs; and provides research information on education issues.

ASCD provides many services to educators—pre-kindergarten through grade 12—as well as to others in the education community, including parents, school board members, administrators, and university professors and students. For more information, contact ASCD via telephone: 1-800-933-2723 or 703-549-9110; fax: 703-299-8631; or

e-mail: member@ascd.org. Or write to ASCD, Information Services, 1250 N. Pitt St., Alexandria, VA 22314-1453 USA. You can find ASCD on the World Wide Web at http://www.ascd.org.

ASCD's Executive Director is Gene R. Carter.

1997-98 ASCD Executive Council

President: Edward Hall, Dean, Division of Social and Professional Studies, Talladega College, Talladega, Alabama

President-Elect: Thomas Budnik, Heartland Area Education Agency, Johnston, Iowa

Immediate Past President: Frances Faircloth Jones, Executive Director, Piedmont Triad Educational Consortium, University of North Carolina, Greensboro, North Carolina

M. Kay Awalt, Associate Superintendent, Franklin Special School District, Franklin, Tennessee

Bonnie Benesh, Change Consultant, Newton, Iowa

Bettye Bobroff, Executive Director, New Mexico ASCD, Albuquerque, New Mexico

Marge Chow, Director, Master in Teaching, City University, Renton, Washington

John Cooper, Assistant Superintendent for Instruction, Canandaigua City School District, Canandaigua, New York

Michael Dzwiniel, Teacher, Edmonton Public Schools, Alberta, Canada

LeRoy Hay, Assistant Superintendent for Instruction, Wallingford Public Schools, Wallingford, Connecticut

Joanna Choi Kalbus, Lecturer in Education, University of California at Riverside, California

Raymond McNulty, Superintendent of Schools, Windham Southeast Supervisory Union, Brattleboro, Vermont

Judy Stevens, Executive Director of Elementary Education, Spring Branch Independent School District, Houston, Texas

Sherrelle J. Walker, Assistant Superintendent, Federal Way School District, Federal Way, Washington

Robert L. Watson, High School Principal, Spearfish 40-2, Spearfish, South Dakota